THE YOUNG PEOPLE'S
ENCYCLOPEDIA
OF THE
UNITED STATES

General Editor: William E. Shapiro

VOLUME 8: PAINE / RODEO

J.G. Ferguson Publishing Company
Chicago, Illinois

This edition published in 1992 for
J.G. Ferguson Publishing Company.

© Grisewood & Dempsey Ltd. and The Millbrook Press Inc., 1992

LIBRARY OF CONGRESS CATALOGING-IN-PUBLICATION DATA

The Young People's Encyclopedia of the United States
p. cm.
Includes index.
Summary: A multivolume encyclopedia with over 1200 alphabetically-
arranged entries covering such topics as the history,
physical features, festivals, and music of the United States
and its neighbors, Mexico and Canada.
ISBN 0-89434-142-1
1. The United States—Encyclopedias. Juvenile.
2. North America—Encyclopedias. Juvenile.
[1. United States—Encyclopedias. 2. North America—Encyclopedias.]
E156.Y68 1992
970.003—dc 20   91–4141
                                                          CIP
                                                          AC
Printed in Italy

THE SUBJECT SYMBOLS

Each entry in this encyclopedia has its own easily recognized symbol opposite the heading. This symbol tells you at a glance which area of interest the entry falls into. Below are the 12 subject areas we have used. At the back of the work there is a list of all the articles divided into subject areas.

HISTORY Events from before colonial times to the present day.

LITERATURE AND THE ARTS Novelists, playwrights, folklore, folk art and crafts, theater, dance, painting, sculpture, architecture of the United States.

PEOPLE AND CULTURE Native and immigrant peoples of North America, their languages and customs, education, health and welfare, social issues.

GEOGRAPHY The land and climate of North America: geographic regions, mountain ranges, rivers and lakes, coastlines, national parks.

SCIENCE AND SPACE Explorations into fields of science and astronomy, famous scientists and innovators.

INDUSTRY AND TECHNOLOGY Transportation, natural resources, manufacturing — industries of yesterday and today.

GOVERNMENT AND LAW The U.S. government, its branches and how it works; the armed services and other governmental organizations; political parties; laws and treaties.

RELIGION, PHILOSOPHY, AND MYTH The wide variety of religious denominations, philosophers and their ideas, myths and legends.

SPORTS AND PASTIMES Baseball, football, basketball, and other sports, sports heroes, plus many hobbies.

COUNTRIES AND PLACES Our neighbors in North and Central America and places of interest.

ANIMALS, PLANTS, AND FOOD North American animals and their habitats, North American plants, agriculture and food, including regional specialities.

STATES AND CITIES Descriptions of each U.S. state, major cities, and sites within and around the country.

The United States depends on freight carried by the trains of the nationwide RAILROAD *system.*

PAINE, Thomas

Thomas Paine (1737–1809) was a political writer and a crusader for democratic rights during the late 1700s.

Born in England, Paine moved to the American colonies in 1774 with the help of Benjamin FRANKLIN. In January 1776 he published a pamphlet called *Common Sense*. It called for American independence from Britain and influenced the men who soon wrote the DECLARATION OF INDEPENDENCE. Paine later wrote a series of pamphlets called *The American Crisis*. These helped boost the morale of the colonial troops.

Paine returned to England in 1787, where he wrote *The Rights of Man*. This book, which supported the French Revolution (1789) and the republican form of government, angered the British government. Paine fled to France, but radical French revolutionaries put him in jail. While there he began to write *The Age of Reason*, which rejected established religion. Paine returned to the United States in 1802.

▲ At the end of the Revolutionary War in 1783, Thomas Paine wrote that "the times that tried men's souls are over."

PAINTED DESERT

The Painted Desert is an area of beautifully colored rocks in the plateau region of north-central ARIZONA. It is a wasteland of mesas, buttes, rock pinnacles, and valleys. But thousands of visitors are drawn to the area, where the pastel colors of the rocks range from red and chocolate to yellow and green.

▼ The Painted Desert extends for 150 miles (240 km) along Arizona's high plateau. Brightly colored cliff faces give the desert its name.

▲ *Charles Gilbert Stuart's unfinished portrait of George Washington was painted in 1796. It is considered the most famous portrait in the United States.*

▶ The Blessing *by Jackson Pollock is an example of abstract expressionism. The artist expresses his feelings by abandoning attempts to depict things realistically.*

▼ *Grant Wood's* American Gothic, *painted in 1930, captures the atmosphere of the Midwest at that time.*

PAINTING

American painting has a history of almost three hundred years. The most popular kind of painting during and following the Colonial period was the portrait. As the country expanded westward in the 1800s, many painters turned their attention to magnificent landscapes and life along the frontier. Toward 1900 prominent American artists drew on European influences to produce realistic paintings. Since the 1930s, however, painters have turned to abstract art.

This encyclopedia contains biographies of many important American painters. Some of them are listed below. You may look up others in the Index.

Some Important Painters of the United States

*Thomas Hart Benton	*Georgia O'Keeffe
Albert Bierstadt	Jackson Pollock
George Caleb Bingham	Frederic Remington
*Mary Cassatt	*Norman Rockwell
George Catlin	*Mark Rothko
*John Singleton Copley	*Albert Pinkham Ryder
Willem de Kooning	*John Singer Sargent
Thomas Eakins	Frank Stella
*Winslow Homer	John Trumbull
*Edward Hopper	*Andy Warhol
*Jasper Johns	Benjamin West
*Rockwell Kent	James A. M. Whistler
Roy Lichtenstein	Grant Wood
*Grandma Moses	Andrew Wyeth
*See individual entries	

 The Paiutes are skilled gatherers of wild fruits and berries. In this photograph, taken early in the 20th-century, Jigger Bob, a 103 year-old Paiute, helps his wife and son to prepare wild cherries.

PAIUTES

The Paiute INDIANS lived in the Great Basin—that area between the Sierra Nevada in the west and the Rocky Mountains in the east. There were two groups of Paiutes, the Southern Paiutes and the Northern Paiutes. The lands of the Southern Paiutes were arid. They lived by gathering seeds, berries, and fruits and by hunting small animals. The lands of the Northern Paiutes were more fruitful. In addition to gathering food and hunting, they also fished. Beginning in the mid-1800s, the Northern Paiutes resisted the white settlers who came to their land. They and the Southern Paiutes were forced onto a number of small reservations in the 1860s and 1870s. Today there are about 5,000 Paiutes.

A Paiute chief called Wovoka had a vision in 1890. It told him to perform a ceremony called the Ghost Dance in order to rid his lands of white people and to fill the plains with buffalo once more. The Ghost Dance movement spread to many other tribes but died out later in 1890 when 200 Indians were wiped out at the Battle of Wounded Knee.

PANAMA CANAL

The Panama Canal links the Atlantic and Pacific oceans. It crosses Central America at its narrowest point, the Isthmus of Panama. Many people in the 1800s had called for a canal so that ships traveling between San Francisco and New York would no longer have to go around the tip of South America. The canal, which opened in 1914, cut about 8,000 miles (13,000 km) from this voyage. The United States built the canal under an agreement with Panama, which had just gained its independence from Colombia. This same agreement, signed in 1903, gave the United States the right to operate the canal and a Canal Zone around it. In 1977, President Jimmy Carter signed a new treaty with Panama. This promised to pass control of the canal to Panama on December 31, 1999.

▼ *The Panama Canal was built across the Isthmus of Panama, one of the narrowest points between North and South America. Engineers reduced the need for digging by running the canal through Lake Gatun.*

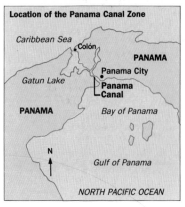

Location of the Panama Canal Zone

Caribbean Sea
Colón
PANAMA
Panama City
Gatun Lake
Panama Canal
PANAMA
Bay of Panama
N
Gulf of Panama
NORTH PACIFIC OCEAN

559

► Dorothy Parker was a noted poet and short-story writer. But many people remember her for her sparkling wit, which typified the lively spirit of the 1920s.

Dorothy Parker had problems falling asleep but refused some advice that friends gave her. "I really can't be expected to drop everything and start counting sheep at my age. I hate sheep."

PARKER, Dorothy

Dorothy Parker (1893–1967) was a literary critic, poet, and short-story writer. Born in West End, New Jersey, she became drama critic for *Vanity Fair* and a book reviewer for the *New Yorker*. Parker was also a member of the Algonquin Round Table. This group of literary and theatrical people met for lunch and witty conversation at New York City's Algonquin Hotel. Parker's short stories appear in *Here Lies* and other collections. Among her volumes of poetry is *Enough Rope*. This book contained one of her wittiest bits of verse: "Men seldom make passes/At girls who wear glasses."

PARKMAN, Francis

Francis Parkman (1823–1893) was a major American historian. His first book, *The Oregon Trail*, was based on his own travels, during which he lived with the Sioux Indians. Despite poor health and weak eyesight, Parkman wrote a multivolume history called *France and England in North America*. This series described the English–French struggle for control of the continent, as well as the role played by American Indians in this struggle. Parkman used original documentation in writing these books.

▼ A passport is an important proof of U.S. citizenship. People should always report a lost or stolen passport.

PASSPORT

A passport is an official government document. It identifies the holder as a citizen of a particular country and allows him or her to travel from one country to another. In the United States, passports are issued by the Passport Services, Bureau of Consular Affairs, U.S. Department of State. It is not necessary to have a passport to visit some countries, such as Canada and Mexico. Other countries may require a *visa*. This is a document or stamp placed in the passport stating that the passport holder's entry has been approved.

PATENTS AND COPYRIGHTS

Governments issue patents to protect the legal and financial rights of inventors. Copyrights protect the rights of creators of literary, musical, and artistic works.

An inventor must apply to the Patent and Trademark Office of the U.S. Department of Commerce. Patents are granted to the first person who actually created the invention. Patents give inventors exclusive rights for 17 years. Only an Act of Congress can renew a patent beyond 17 years.

Authors have copyright for the whole of their lifetime. This is extended for another 50 years after their death. This allows heirs to benefit from payments for the work. For works created before 1978, the copyright

Patents Issued (1980–1988)	
1980	66,200
1981	71,000
1982	63,300
1983	62,000
1984	72,700
1985	77,200
1986	76,900
1987	89,400
1988	84,300

Top Copyrights
1. Musical works
2. Computer software
3. Works of visual art
4. Renewals

The first U.S. patent was issued in 1790 to Samuel Hopkins of Vermont for making "pot ash and pearl ash by a new apparatus and process." Since then more than 4 million patents have been issued— about 70,000 a year. Thomas Edison obtained more than 1,000 patents.

◄ Elisha Otis built the first elevator with protective safety devices. He demonstrated his invention at a fair in New York City in 1854.

is 28 years and can now be renewed for another 47 years. Copyrights are registered by the Copyright Office of the LIBRARY OF CONGRESS.

In the 1930s, Alice Paul worked with several international women's organizations. In 1938 she founded the World Women's Party.

PAUL, Alice

Alice Paul (1885–1977) was a leader of the American WOMEN'S RIGHTS movement. Born in Moorestown, New Jersey, she lived in England from 1907 to 1910. While there she became involved in the British suffragette movement. Upon returning to the United States, Paul organized marches and protest meetings, demanding that women be allowed to vote. She founded and was chairperson of the National Woman's Party. After the passage, in 1920, of the Nineteenth Amendment, which gave women the right to vote, Paul continued working for another amendment to give women equal rights in other areas. She submitted the first version of this amendment to Congress in 1923 and continued working for women's rights into the 1960s.

PAULING, Linus

The chemist Linus Pauling (1901–) was the second person (after Marie Curie) to win two Nobel Prizes. He won the 1954 Nobel Prize for chemistry for his work on the structure of molecules, the basic units of chemical compounds, and the forces that bind them together. He also won the 1962 Nobel Peace Prize for campaigning against the testing of atomic weapons. Pauling advocates the use of high doses of vitamin C to combat the common cold. Many consider this treatment to be controversial. Born in Portland, Oregon, Pauling taught at the California Institute of Technology.

▼ Religion was very important to the Pawnees. One annual ceremony involved sacrificing a young woman. She was meant as a gift and to carry messages to the gods. According to legend, this ritual stopped when Petalshara, a Pawnee, rescued a Comanche girl who was meant to be sacrificed and took her back to her own tribe. When he returned, unharmed, he proved to the Pawnee tribe that human sacrifice was not necessary.

PAWNEES

The Pawnees once lived along the Platte River in Nebraska. They were farmers, growing crops of maize (corn) and beans, but twice a year they hunted buffalo on the plains. In 1857 the Pawnees moved onto a reservation in Nebraska. But they soon faced pressure from white settlers and attacks by hostile Indian tribes. They were moved to Indian Territory (Oklahoma) in 1875. Today there are about 2,000 Pawnees. Many live in and around Pawnee, Oklahoma.

PEACE CORPS

The Peace Corps is an independent agency of the United States government. Its most important goal is to help developing countries train people in such areas as agriculture, health, education, natural-resource conservation, and the development of small businesses. By doing this, the Peace Corps helps promote world peace and friendship and increases understanding between the United States and the host countries. John F. Kennedy promised to develop a Peace Corps when he ran for president. Its establishment, in March 1961, was one of his first acts as president. Today there are more than 6,000 Peace Corps volunteers in 73 countries in Latin America, Africa, Asia, the Pacific, and parts of Eastern Europe. Before being sent overseas, volunteers are trained for 9 to 14 weeks.

PEANUT

The peanut is not a nut but a type of pea. It is an important crop, and the United States is one of the world's leading producers. Peanuts grow only in warmer regions. Georgia is the largest peanut-growing state. Alabama, North Carolina, Texas, and Virginia are also important producers. About half of the U.S. harvest is used to make peanut butter. About a quarter is sold as roasted nuts. Only a small proportion is crushed for oil, although this is the main use for peanuts outside the United States. Peanuts are also used as livestock feed. George Washington CARVER discovered many uses for the peanut.

▲ A U.S. Peace Corps volunteer helps install an irrigation system in Senegal. During his two years of service he will pass on his knowledge so local people can take over from him.

▼ Peanuts have many uses. They can be cooked to prepare foods such as peanut brittle and peanut butter. Processing (breaking up) peanuts releases oil that can be used for shampoo and even paint.

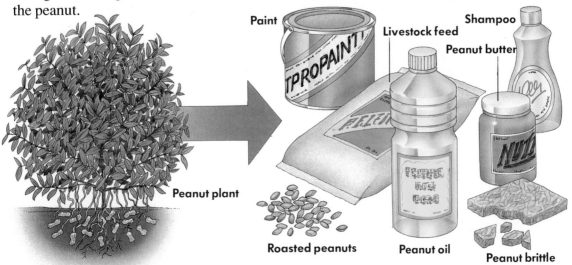

Peanut plant

Paint

Livestock feed

Shampoo

Peanut butter

Roasted peanuts

Peanut oil

Peanut brittle

► *Eight battleships were destroyed when Japanese airplanes bombed the U.S. naval base at Pearl Harbor on December 7, 1941. Some 2,400 U.S. sailors and soldiers died in the attack.*

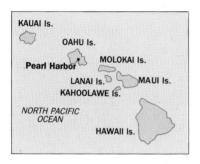

▼ *Robert E. Peary set off for the North Pole in 1909 from Ellesmere Island in northern Canada. He and his team built an igloo when they reached the North Pole on April 6, 1909.*

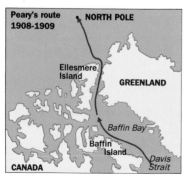

PEARL HARBOR

Pearl Harbor, located on the island of Oahu, Hawaii, has been the home base of the United States Pacific Fleet since 1940. In the early morning hours of December 7, 1941, Japanese carrier-based airplanes attacked Pearl Harbor. More than 2,400 American soldiers and sailors were killed, and 18 major ships were destroyed or seriously damaged. The Japanese lost fewer than 100 men. On the following day, after President Franklin D. ROOSEVELT called December 7 "a date which will live in infamy," the Congress declared war on Japan, and the United States entered WORLD WAR II. "Remember Pearl Harbor!" was the United States' rallying cry until the defeat of Japan in 1945.

PEARY, Robert E.

Admiral Robert Peary (1856–1920) led the first expedition to reach the North Pole. During the late 1880s and early 1890s, he made five trips to Greenland. On one expedition, he traveled by sledge over 1,300 miles (2,100 km) of ice and snow and proved that Greenland was an island. He then made several attempts to reach the Pole, finally succeeding in 1909 along with his black companion Matthew Henson and four Eskimos. Peary wrote several books about his expeditions, including *The North Pole* and *Secrets of Polar Travel*.

PECOS BILL

Pecos Bill is a legendary cowboy hero. He was created by the writer Edward O'Reilly in 1923. The character soon became a hero of American FOLKLORE. It was said that Pecos Bill was born in Texas in the 1830s and was reared by coyotes along the Pecos River. According to legend, he invented all the cowboys' techniques, including roping and branding. Among the tall tales told about him is how he once rode a tornado from Oklahoma to California, where he crash-landed, creating Death Valley. The heavy rain that washed away the tornado was said to have formed the Grand Canyon.

PELICAN

A WATER BIRD, the pelican is one of the largest birds with webbed feet. It nests in large colonies on rivers, lakes, and coasts. The American white pelican is common in western North America, nesting on islands in lakes from Canada south to Texas. It spends the winter on the California coast, on the Gulf coast, in the South, or in the Caribbean. The brown pelican is found in coastal regions of the Southeast and California, particularly in reserves such as Pelican Island in Florida.

PENN, William

William Penn (1644–1788) was the founder of the colony of PENNSYLVANIA. Throughout his life, he was a supporter of civil and religious rights.

Penn was born in London, England. His father was a vice admiral of the English fleet and a member of the ruling classes. Penn, however, joined the Quakers (see FRIENDS, SOCIETY OF) while in his early twenties. In England, at that time, Quakers were persecuted, and Penn spent some time in prison.

In 1681, to pay off a debt to Penn's father, King Charles II gave Penn a charter for a colony in the Americas. It was named Pennsylvania after Penn's father. Penn took Quakers and other settlers there in 1682 and built a prosperous colony. There was religious freedom in the colony, and the people set up a representative assembly. Penn established friendly relations with the Indians in the area. He lived in Pennsylvania from 1682 to 1684 and 1699 to 1701.

▲ The legendary western character Pecos Bill could ride a tornado as he would ride a bucking bronco. According to the story, Death Valley was formed from the hole where he crashed.

▼ William Penn was granted the land that became Pennsylvania because British King Charles II owed Penn's father money. The king was relieved when Penn took other Quakers with him to America.

Mountain laurel

Ruffed grouse

Hemlock

Pennsylvania is a state in the northeastern United States. It borders Lake Erie and is an important industrial, agricultural, and mining state. It is also a historic one. Pennsylvania was one of the original 13 colonies and the second state to join the Union. Because of its central location in the new American nation—six states were to the north and six to the south—Pennsylvania was nicknamed the Keystone State.

The APPALACHIAN Highlands cover most of Pennsylvania, but there are many areas of plains and valleys with farms. Corn, oats, soybeans, and mushrooms are important agricultural products. Among the state's manufactured goods are petroleum products, drugs, motor vehicles, and electronic goods. But the state is best known for its steel. PITTSBURG, in the western part of the state, is the leading steel city in the United States. Pennsylvania's mineral products include portland cement, stone, pig iron, and lime. PHILADELPHIA, the largest city, is a major port on the Delaware River.

The colony of Pennsylvania was founded in 1682 by William PENN as a haven for Quakers. For this reason, Pennsylvania is sometimes called the Quaker State. The Continental Congress met in Philadelphia and directed the American Revolution from there. The Battle of GETTYSBURG and other battles were fought in Pennsylvania during the Civil War. It was also at Gettysburg that President Abraham Lincoln gave his famous GETTYSBURG ADDRESS.

Pennsylvania

Capital: Harrisburg
Area: 44,888 sq mi (116,260 km²). Rank: 32nd
Population: 11,924,710 (1990). **Rank:** 5th
Statehood: Dec. 12, 1787
Principal rivers: Allegheny, Susquehanna, Delaware, Ohio
Highest point: Mt. Davis, 3,213 ft (979 m)
Motto: Virtue, Liberty, and Independence
Song: None

▶ *An Amish buggy travels along a road near Lancaster, in the heart of Pennsylvania Dutch country. The Amish believe that it is wrong to use many modern inventions.*

▲ Cable cars in Pittsburgh take passengers up and down the steep hills by the riverbank.

Places of Interest
● Gettysburg National Military Park was the scene of the famous Battle of Gettysburg during the Civil War and the place where Abraham Lincoln delivered his Gettysburg Address.
● Philadelphia, originally the country's capital, is full of interesting sites. The Declaration of Independence and the Constitution were both adopted in the historic Independence Hall.
● The Appalachian Mountains run through the state and provide sites for many activities, including camping, fishing, and skiing.

▲ Freshly harvested pumpkins are prepared for shipment. Pennsylvania is one of the leading farming states east of the Mississippi River.

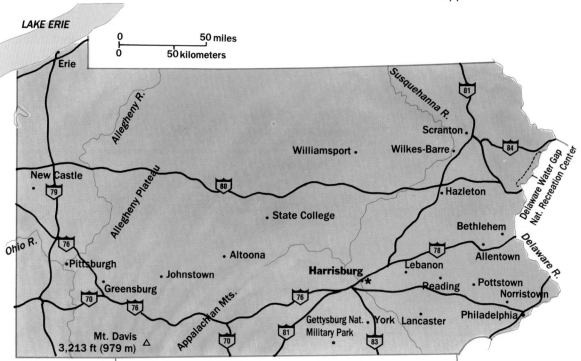

▲ *During the Battle of Lake Erie, in the War of 1812, Oliver Perry's ship, the* Lawrence, *was severely damaged. Perry rowed to another ship in his fleet, the* Niagara. *Under Perry's command the* Niagara *quickly defeated the British ships.*

▼ *General John Pershing was known as "Black Jack" because he led black troops during the Mexican campaign of 1916.*

PERRY, Matthew C. and Oliver H.

Matthew C. and Oliver Hazard Perry, brothers, were famous American naval officers. Oliver (1785–1819), the eldest, fought in the WAR OF 1812. He commanded a naval force on Lake Erie, where his fleet defeated the British. Perry sent a famous message to his commander, announcing, "We have met the enemy and they are ours." Matthew Perry (1794–1858) is known as the man who opened Japan to the rest of the world. In 1853 he sailed a fleet of American ships into Tokyo Bay. In the following year he signed a treaty with Japan that gave the United States trading rights with that country.

PERSHING, John J.

John Joseph "Black Jack" Pershing (1860–1948) was the commander of the American Expeditionary Forces (AEF) in WORLD WAR I. Pershing was born in Laclede, Missouri. He graduated from West Point in 1886 and became a cavalry officer. His first battle experience was against the Apache Indians. He later fought in the Spanish-American War (1898) and in the Philippines. In 1916, Pershing led U.S. troops against the Mexican revolutionary leader Pancho Villa, who had raided some American towns. In 1917, Pershing was named commander of the AEF. His 2 million troops played an important part in defeating Germany in World War I. After the war he was promoted to the newly created rank of general of the armies.

PERSIAN GULF WAR

The 1991 Persian Gulf War pitted Iraq against a U.S.-led coalition. These allied forces were commanded by U.S. General H. Norman SCHWARZKOPF. The war forced Iraq to withdraw from Kuwait, which it had invaded and occupied on August 2, 1990. Allied air attacks on Iraqi targets began on January 16, 1991. The ground war started on February 23. Iraq was defeated in four days. Sophisticated electronic weapons systems played a major role in the war. The allied military death toll was less than 200. Iraq lost 25,000 to 50,000 troops.

The Persian Gulf War started one day after the deadline President George Bush set for an Iraqi withdrawal from Kuwait. President Bush called the January 15 deadline ''a line drawn in the sand.'' Iraq stepped across that line —and brought on the fighting—by continuing to occupy Kuwait.

◀ Elfreth's Alley in Philadelphia. Many streets in the city's older districts look unchanged from the 1790s, when Philadelphia was the nation's capital.

PHILADELPHIA

With a population of almost 1.6 million, Philadelphia is the largest city in PENNSYLVANIA and the fifth largest city in the United States. It is known as the birthplace of the nation. The DECLARATION OF INDEPENDENCE was signed there. The U.S. CONSTITUTION was drafted there. And the LIBERTY BELL, symbol of American independence, is in Liberty Bell Pavilion in Independence National Historical Park.

Philadelphia was founded by William PENN in 1682. It was the capital of the United States from 1790 to 1800. Today, as in Colonial times, it is an important port on the Delaware River, in southeastern Pennsylvania. It is also an important commercial, banking, and educational center. Textiles, chemicals, and petroleum products are among the city's manufactures.

Philadelphia's population of almost 1.6 million makes it the fifth largest city in the United States. But, like other major East Coast cities, it is not growing as fast as those in the Sun Belt. Philadelphia was ranked third in 1950: since then it has been overtaken by Los Angeles and Houston.

▼ *The architecture of St. Mary's Basilica in Phoenix shows the Spanish influence on the American Southwest.*

Important American Photographers
Berenice Abbott
*Ansel Adams
Diane Arbus
Richard Avedon
*Margaret Bourke-White
*Mathew Brady
Harry Callahan
Robert Capa
Walker Evans
Robert Frank
Lee Friedlander
Ernst Haas
William Jackson
Dorothea Lange
Irving Penn
Eliot Porter
Jacob A. Riis
W. Eugene Smith
*Edward Steichen
*Alfred Stieglitz
Jerry Velsmann
Edward Weston
Minor White
Garry Winogrand
*See individual entries

▶ *Dorothea Lange's photographs documented some of the hardest times in the Depression.*

PHOENIX

Phoenix is the capital of ARIZONA and its largest city. It has a population of 983,000. The city is located on the Salt River, in the south-central part of the state.

Gold prospectors who arrived in 1867 were the first white settlers. The city experienced a boom after World War II, when air-conditioning made life easier in the hot climate. Today, Phoenix's clean, dry air and sunny days attract many new settlers. The city is an important center for the manufacture of aerospace and electronic equipment.

PHOTOGRAPHY

Photography is the art of taking pictures with cameras. These pictures, called photographs, have many uses. One of their most important uses is to communicate information. Photographs used in books, magazines, and newspapers, as well as in advertisements, are among this type. Many photographs are considered works of art, just like paintings.

Photography developed primarily in France and England during the early 1800s. But it was the American inventor George EASTMAN who made picture taking simple enough for amateurs. In 1888 he invented the Kodak box camera, the first camera to use rolls of film. Before that, pictures were taken using glass plates.

American photographers were active during the mid-1800s. William Henry Jackson photographed the American West. Mathew BRADY became famous for his Civil War photographs. One of the most famous war photographers of this century was Robert Capa, who photographed some of the battles of World War II. Some photographers have used the camera to point out social problems. Dorothea Lange's pictures of migrant workers during the Great Depression are among the outstanding examples of this.

Alfred STIEGLITZ, Edward STEICHEN, and Ansel ADAMS are among the many photographers who have explored the artistic possibilities of the camera.

▲ Young photographers discover that using a camera can be exciting and fun. Many schools have camera clubs where students can learn new techniques and even develop their own pictures.

◄ This Walker Evans photograph captured the spirit of a southern dry goods store in the 1930s.

▼ Mary Pickford kept her popular screen image as an innocent beauty. In real life she was an able businesswoman and helped found United Artists, a major movie studio.

PICKFORD, Mary

Mary Pickford (1893–1979) was a silent movie star. She was born in Canada but spent most of her life in Hollywood. Pickford was widely liked and became known as "America's Sweetheart." She was in 194 motion pictures from 1909 until her retirement in 1933. In 1929 she won the ACADEMY AWARD for best actress for her role in *Coquette.* Her other popular films included *Rebecca of Sunnybrook Farm, Pollyana, Little Lord Fauntleroy,* and *Little Annie Rooney.* She was one of the founding members of the United Artists movie studio. Mary Pickford married Douglas FAIRBANKS, Sr., in 1920.

Franklin Pierce was the 14th president of the United States. He served from 1853 to 1857, a period of worsening relations between the North and South over the issue of slavery.

Pierce, a Democrat and a lawyer, served in the New Hampshire legislature from 1829 to 1833 and in the U.S. House of Representatives and Senate from 1833 to 1842. In 1852 the Democrats chose Pierce as a compromise candidate for the presidential nomination. He was a Northerner, but Southerners also trusted him because he had supported the Compromise of 1850, including the Fugitive Slave Law. In the election, Pierce defeated his Whig opponent Winfield Scott.

As president, Pierce supported the Kansas-Nebraska Act (1854). It created two new territories—Kansas and Nebraska—and allowed settlers to choose whether or

▲ The Kansas-Nebraska Act caused heated discussions and violence among the people of those states.

Franklin Pierce
Born: November 23, 1804, in Hillsboro, New Hampshire
Education: Bowdoin College
Political party: Democratic
Term of office: 1853–1857
Married: 1834 to Jane Appleton
Died: October 8, 1869, in Concord, New Hampshire

not they wanted slavery in the territory. Soon, pro- and anti-slavery groups in Kansas were fighting bitter battles, and the United States moved closer to civil war.

Pierce followed an aggressive foreign policy. He called for the annexation of Hawaii and the takeover of Cuba. His major accomplishment was the GADSDEN PURCHASE (1853). The United States acquired a strip of land from Mexico that forms the southern parts of Arizona and New Mexico. In 1854 the United States and Japan signed a treaty opening Japanese ports to American trade.

Pierce's handling of the slavery issue made him very unpopular. He was not chosen as the Democratic candidate in the 1856 presidential election.

PIGEON

Of the 300 species of wild pigeons in the world, 11 are found in the United States and 3 in Canada. Smaller pigeons are known as doves. One of the smallest is the American ground dove, which is about 6 inches (15 cm) long. The largest wild pigeon in the United States is the band-tailed pigeon, a favorite game bird in the West. The most common is the mourning dove; its name refers to the male's mournful, cooing love song.

A number of breeds of domestic pigeons are bred as a hobby or business. The most popular breed for meat is the white king pigeon. Homing pigeons are bred for racing and carrying messages. Carrier pigeons also carry messages. Fancy breeds raised for shows include the pouter pigeon. The street pigeons found in cities are descended from domestic breeds.

▲ The feathers of most pigeons are dull black, blue, brown, or gray. Pigeons are strong fliers and are sometimes used to carry messages to faraway places.

PIGS AND HOGS

In the United States pigs weighing more than 120 pounds (50 kg) are called hogs. The United States is one of the top three pig- and hog-raising countries. Iowa is the leading pig- and hog-raising state. Because corn is their main food, more than two thirds of pigs and hogs produced in the United States are raised in the Corn Belt states of the Midwest. About 20 breeds of pigs are raised, most of which were developed in the United States.

The only wild pig or hog found on the continent is the razorback hog, from the swamps of the South.

▼ Some breeds of pigs are well suited to the American climate and eating habits. There are more than 53 million pigs on U.S. farms.

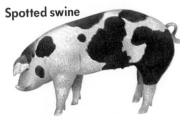

Spotted swine

American landrace

Poland china

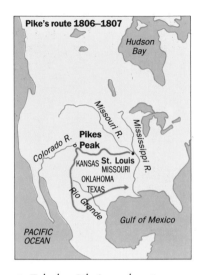

Pike's route 1806–1807

Hudson Bay

Missouri R.

Pikes Peak

Colorado R.

Mississippi R.

KANSAS St. Louis
MISSOURI

OKLAHOMA

TEXAS

Rio Grande

PACIFIC OCEAN

Gulf of Mexico

▲ Zebulon Pike's explorations helped to open up the Southwest.

PIKE, Zebulon

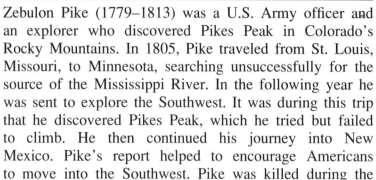

Zebulon Pike (1779–1813) was a U.S. Army officer and an explorer who discovered Pikes Peak in Colorado's Rocky Mountains. In 1805, Pike traveled from St. Louis, Missouri, to Minnesota, searching unsuccessfully for the source of the Mississippi River. In the following year he was sent to explore the Southwest. It was during this trip that he discovered Pikes Peak, which he tried but failed to climb. He then continued his journey into New Mexico. Pike's report helped to encourage Americans to move into the Southwest. Pike was killed during the War of 1812.

PILGRIMS See Plymouth Colony; Puritans

PINE

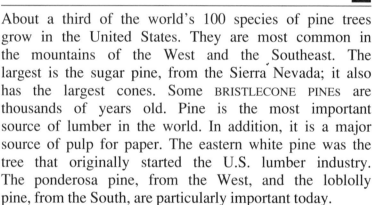

About a third of the world's 100 species of pine trees grow in the United States. They are most common in the mountains of the West and the Southeast. The largest is the sugar pine, from the Sierra Nevada; it also has the largest cones. Some BRISTLECONE PINES are thousands of years old. Pine is the most important source of lumber in the world. In addition, it is a major source of pulp for paper. The eastern white pine was the tree that originally started the U.S. lumber industry. The ponderosa pine, from the West, and the loblolly pine, from the South, are particularly important today.

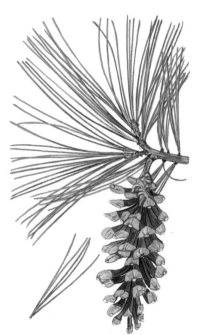

▲ A white pine is easy to identify. Its needles are clustered in groups of five, matching the number of letters in the word white.

▶ This California pine forest has just been hit by a storm. Some types of pine trees have shallow roots. They can be overturned easily by strong winds.

PIONEERS

Pioneers are people who are the first to settle in a particular territory. In United States history, the word *pioneer* is especially used to describe those people who were part of the WESTWARD MOVEMENT. During this movement, which began in the mid-1700s and ended more than a century later, people from the East moved west to settle the rest of the continent.

Even as American colonists were fighting the British at the battles of LEXINGTON AND CONCORD, Daniel BOONE was blazing a trail across the Appalachian Mountains. Soon, pioneers were crossing the mountains to settle in Kentucky, Tennessee, and the Ohio Valley. The second great wave of pioneers began to make their way west after the War of 1812. By the 1840s, using the OREGON TRAIL and other trails, they were crossing the

▲ *Decorative Dutch ceramic tiles depicted the Pilgrims' voyage of 1620. Many of the Pilgrims had first moved to Holland to escape religious conflict in England.*

◀ *Pilgrims believed in the importance of Bible studies. Families devoted much of their time to Scripture study and prayers.*

▼ *Clearing a plot of land out of woods was the first job of the earliest pioneers. The timber could then be used to build log cabins.*

Great Plains in record numbers. The destination for many of them was the west coast—California and Oregon. This dangerous journey of 2,000 miles (3,200 km) often took six months. These pioneers, many of them in wagon trains, faced Indian attacks, diseases, and other hardships. But the lure of fertile farmland and a new life drew them to the West.

Newcomers at a frontier settlement often lived in the stockade—a wooden fort—until they could build their own log cabins and clear the land to make farms.

The era of the pioneers ended around 1890, when Oklahoma was opened to homesteaders.

► *Pirates would take their stolen cargoes to hideouts along the southeast coast of America. Even today people search for buried pirate treasure on the islands off the coast of South Carolina and Georgia.*

Pittsburgh has over 720 bridges — more than any other U.S. city. Radio station KDKA of Pittsburgh began broadcasting in 1920, the first regular commercial radio station in the United States.

▼ *A modern greenhouse flanks the base of One PPG Place, which rises 635 feet (193 m) above Pittsburgh's commercial district.*

PIRATES AND BUCCANEERS

During the period of colonization in the New World, many pirates, or buccaneers, preyed on ships and settlements in the Americas. The most famous of them was the British buccaneer Henry Morgan (1635–1688), who led raids on town in the West Indies and South and Central America. Another British pirate was Edward Teach (?–1718), known as Blackbeard, who attacked towns along the coast of Virginia and the Carolinas.

In the late 1700s, American merchant ships in the Mediterranean were sometimes captured by the Barbary pirates of Tripoli and other North African states. Between 1801 and 1805 the United States and Tripoli fought a naval war over the issue. The most famous American pirate was Jean Laffite (1780?–1825?). During the War of 1812, he and his band of pirates and smugglers helped Andrew JACKSON defeat the British at the Battle of New Orleans.

PITTSBURGH

With a population of 369,879, Pittsburgh is the second largest city in Pennsylvania. It is located in the western part of the state, where the Monongahela and Allegheny rivers join to form the Ohio River.

Pittsburgh is an important industrial and transportation center and the steel capital of the United States since the late 1800s. Pittsburgh factories also produce glassware, machinery, oil products, and chemicals.

PLAINS INDIANS

The Plains INDIANS lived on the grasslands of North America for thousands of years. This vast area stretched from the Mississippi River in the east to the Rocky Mountains in the west and from Canada in the north to Texas in the south.

Until the 1600s, many Plains tribes were farmers. They grew maize (corn), beans, and other foods, but they also hunted buffalo on foot, using bows and arrows. Beginning in the 1600s, the Indian way of life on the plains was changed when the Spanish introduced the horse. With horses, the Indians could follow the buffalo with ease. The buffalo provided the Indians with meat. Tools and weapons were made from the animals' bones. And tepees and clothing were made from their skins.

As the use of horses became more widespread, many nomadic hunting tribes, such as the APACHES, CHEYENNES, COMANCHES, and SIOUX, entered the plains to hunt buffalo. They fought each other and the tribes that had farmed on the plains. And, beginning in the 1840s, they fought American settlers who were heading west across the Indian hunting grounds.

In the late 1800s, American hunters killed millions of buffalo. The Indians, without their main source of food, suffered greatly. Fierce battles with American soldiers resulted in the deaths of thousands of Plains Indians. Their last battle was the Battle of Wounded Knee in South Dakota in 1890. U.S. soldiers slaughtered 200 Sioux. Soon, the Indians were moved onto reservations. The way of life of the Plains Indians was over.

Tribes of the Great Plains
Arapaho
Assiniboin
Atakapa
Blackfoot
Caddo
Cheyenne
Comanche
Crow
Gros Ventre
Iowa
Kiowa
Mandan
Osage
Pawnee
Ponca
Quapaw
Sioux
Wichita

Many Plains Indians tribes had had 250 years of contact with the Spanish by the time the first Americans entered their territory. The Indians' fighting tactics and good horsemanship helped them secure some notable victories against the U.S. Army.

◀ Plains Indian hunters often wore coyote skins in order to sneak up to a herd of buffalo without startling them. Sioux Hunting the Buffalo, by George Catlin, captures the tension of the hunt.

PLANT LIFE

▲ Grasslands like these in Missouri once covered the land that became the rich farming regions of the Midwest.

▼ Bear grass thrives on the upper slopes of Glacier National Park in Montana. Few other plants can survive the harsh climate and short growing season.

There are about 400,000 kinds of plants in the world. Many thousands of these are native to North America.

Forests cover about 728 million acres (295 million ha) of land in the United States. In the East, forests contain both hardwood and softwood trees, including PINE, OAK, birch, beech, walnut, hickory, and MAPLE. Oak, maple, hickory, walnut, and ash trees grow in some parts of the central United States. Grassland once covered much of the central United States—the PRAIRIES and the GREAT PLAINS. Now much of this land is used for farming and for grazing cattle.

Along the Gulf coast, pine, hickory, pecan, gum, syca-more, and birch trees are common. Southern Florida, especially, has tropical trees such as the palm. Giant redwoods and SEQUOIAS and Douglas firs grow along the Pacific coast. CACTUSES, yucca, and Joshua trees survive in the dry areas of the Southwest.

WILDFLOWERS grow in almost all areas. The lady's slipper and the JACK-IN-THE-PULPIT are common woodland flowers. Daisies, pink roses, black-eyed Susans, and Queen Anne's lace are found in meadows. And flowers of the prairies include poppies, sunflowers, and verbena. Phlox and harebells grow high up in the mountains, and the deserts are home to desert marigolds, desert lilies, Arizona poppies, and the flowers of various cactuses. Among the water plants in the United States are water lilies, marsh marigolds, and cattails. And in the far north, poppies and other hardy flowers appear during the brief spring.

Natural Plant Life of U.S. Regions

East: Mainly deciduous forest; pine forests in Southeast; tropical swamps in Florida.

Midwest: Grasslands in the Corn Belt and Plains states; coniferous forests in north.

Southwest: Desert plants such as cactuses and deep-rooted shrubs.

Rockies: Mixture of all types, depending on elevation.

West Coast: Ranges from evergreen forests in north to subtropical plants in south.

Hawaii: Rain forests, coconut palm groves.

Alaska: Tundra in north; evergreen forests in south.

▲ *Cactuses cover desert areas in the Southwest. Some cactuses produce strikingly beautiful flowers.*

▼ *Fungi at Monterey Bay, California. Most fungi grow in damp, forested places.*

▼ *Water lilies grow from the mud bottom of shallow water. They grow in both temperate and hot climates.*

▲ *Plimoth Plantation in Massachusetts is a reconstruction of the first Pilgrim settlement. The Mayflower II, a replica of the original Mayflower, is moored in the background.*

▼ *Published editions of Edgar Allan Poe's works often contained vivid illustrations. This woodcut appeared in a version of* The Raven.

PLYMOUTH COLONY

Plymouth Colony was the second permanent English colony in America. It was founded in 1620 by PURITANS who sailed from England aboard the *Mayflower*. They landed at the site of the famous Plymouth rock in Massachusetts. These Puritans—who called themselves Pilgrims—were seeking religious freedom. The first year in America was a difficult one for the Pilgrims. But things improved when MASSASOIT, chief of the local Wampanoag Indians, befriended them. In 1621 the Pilgrims and Indians celebrated the first American THANKSGIVING together. William Bradford was governor of the colony between 1621 and 1656. In the 1670s, however, Massasoit's son began what is known as King Philip's War. More than a thousand New England colonists were killed. In 1692, Plymouth Colony became part of the Massachusetts Bay Colony.

POCAHONTAS

Pocahontas (1595?–1617) was the daughter of the Indian chief POWHATAN. According to John Smith, one of the founders of the JAMESTOWN Settlement in Virginia, Pocahontas saved his life. Powhatan was about to kill him. In 1613, Pocahontas was taken captive by the Jamestown colonists. During her captivity she became a Christian and took the name Rebecca. The following year she married James Rolfe, a tobacco planter. This began a period of peace between the Indians and colonists. Pocahontas traveled to England with her husband in 1616. She became ill and died there the following year.

POE, Edgar Allan

The poet and story writer Edgar Allan Poe (1809–1849) is best known for his tales of mystery and horror.

Born in Boston, Poe was educated in England and Virginia. He worked as an editor and writer on several literary magazines. It was in one of these that his story "The Fall of the House of Usher" first appeared in 1839. His detective story "The Murders in the Rue Morgue" was first published in another. Among Poe's best horror stories are "The Tell-Tale Heart" and "The Pit and the Pendulum." One of his best poems is "The Raven."

POETRY

Much of American poetry has changed with the course of American history. During the Colonial period, those seeking religious freedom in the New World wrote about religious subjects. Patriotic poems, such as Joel Barlow's *The Vision of Columbus*, were popular during and after the Revolutionary War period. And poems about nature by William Cullen BRYANT and other poets were popular during the first half of the 1800s.

American themes were the subjects of poems written as the nation expanded westward during the middle to late 1800s and civil war erupted. Among them were Henry Wadsworth LONGFELLOW's *Song of Hiawatha* and John Greenleaf WHITTIER's anti-slavery collection of poems, *Voices of Freedom*. Ralph Waldo EMERSON and Walt WHITMAN were others whose poetry was about America and Americans. Whitman's collection of poems, *Leaves of Grass*, is considered one of the world's most important literary works.

The 1900s brought new subjects to American poetry. Some poets began writing about things European, and black Americans such as Countee CULLEN and Langston HUGHES created poetry about the black experience in America. More recently, some American poets, such as Robert LOWELL and Sylvia Plath, have tended to write poems about personal experiences.

▼ Three great American poets of the 20th century. Carl Sandburg won the 1951 Pulitzer Prize for poetry; Sylvia Plath and Ezra Pound produced personal visions that touched readers around the world.

Carl Sandburg

Sylvia Plath

Ezra Pound

Some Important American Poets

Conrad Aiken
W. H. Auden
*Steven Vincent Benét
John Berryman
*Gwendolyn Brooks
William Cullen Bryant
Countee Cullen
E. E. Cummings
*Emily Dickinson
*Ralph Waldo Emerson
*Robert Frost
*Frances Harper
*Oliver Wendell Holmes
*Langston Hughes
Vachel Lindsay
*Henry Wadsworth Longfellow
Amy Lowell
*James Russell Lowell
Robert Lowell
Archibald MacLeish

Edna St. Vincent Millay
*Marianne Moore
Ogden Nash
*Dorothy Parker
Sylvia Plath
*Edgar Allan Poe
*Ezra Pound
John Crowe Ransom
Adrienne Rich
James Whitcomb Riley
*Edwin A. Robinson
Theodore Roethke
*Carl Sandburg
*Wallace Stevens
John Updike
Robert Penn Warren
*Walt Whitman
*John Greenleaf Whittier
Richard Wilbur
William Carlos Williams

*See individual entries

Some Poisonous Plants
Holly berry
Jimsonweed
Poison hemlock
Poison ivy
Poison oak
Poison sumac
Spider lily
Star-of-Bethlehem
Tiger lily

Some Venomous Animals
Black widow spider
Copperhead snake
Portuguese man-of-war
Rattlesnake
Scorpionfish
Tick
Water moccasin snake

► *Some poisonous plants and animals, such as the foxglove and the copperhead snake, can cause death. A poison ivy rash or a tarantula bite is painful but not fatal.*

▼ *In the movie* In the Heat of the Night, *Sidney Poitier played a policeman who had to work with a white racist colleague.*

POISONOUS PLANTS AND ANIMALS

About 700 kinds of plants found in North America are poisonous. Some are deadly. Others just cause illness. Some are poisonous when eaten. Among the poisonous North American plants are aconite, belladonna (deadly nightshade), water hemlock, LOCOWEED, and poisonous MUSHROOMS. Even some garden plants are poisonous. Some of these are daphne, foxglove, mountain laurel, larkspur, hydrangea, lily of the valley, wisteria, and rhododendron. Some plants, such as poison ivy, poison oak, poison sumac, and poinsettias, are poisonous when they are touched.

North American animals that have poisonous bites or stings include BEES, wasps, and hornets; some scorpions; the brown spider and black widow spider; certain ANTS; the Gila monster; copperheads, RATTLESNAKES, and water moccasins; and the short-tailed shrew.

Common foxglove

Poison ivy

American tarantula

Copperhead

POITIER, Sidney

Sidney Poitier (1927–) is an important movie actor. Born in Miami, Florida, and raised in the Bahamas, he moved to New York in the 1940s and studied acting. His fine talent on the stage soon brought him to Hollywood. Many of his films center around the problems of being black in the United States. In *Guess Who's Coming to Dinner* his character meets the parents of the white woman to whom he is engaged. In the film *In the Heat of the Night* he plays a northern policeman in a bigoted southern town during a murder investigation.

POLAR REGIONS

The polar regions are the regions around the North Pole and South Pole. They are the two coldest areas in the world.

The north polar region consists of the land and water within the Arctic Circle. In North America, it includes the northern parts of Alaska and Canada's Yukon Territory and Northwest Territories. Few people other than Inuits (Eskimos) and miners live in these lands. But the north polar region is rich in minerals. And most of Alaska's oil is from its Arctic coastline.

The south polar region consists of the area south of the Antarctic Circle. Most of this area is taken up by the frozen continent of Antarctica. The United States, as well as other countries, has year-round scientific stations there. In 1959 the United States and other countries signed the Antarctic Treaty. They promised that "Antarctica shall be used for peaceful purposes only."

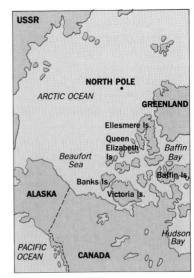

▲ The polar ice cap, made up of frozen water of the Arctic Ocean, covers the North Pole. The South Pole is covered by Antarctica, one of the seven continents.

◄ U.S. polar research stations, such as the Amundsen-Scott Station in Antarctica, measure wind speeds, temperature, and snowfall. They contribute valuable information about the earth's climate and atmosphere.

▼ A policewoman patrols 42nd Street, one of the busiest areas of New York City.

POLICE

The job of the police is to maintain public order. Police, or law enforcement, officers prevent crimes, protect people and their property, and enforce laws. There are more than 20,000 law enforcement agencies and almost 800,000 law enforcement officers in the United States.

The FEDERAL BUREAU OF IVESTIGATION (FBI) is the best known federal law enforcement agency. There are more than 115,000 state police officers. They patrol state highways. The 600,000 local police officers work for counties, cities, and other municipalities.

Some Third Parties
in United States History
Prohibition Party (founded 1869) fought to outlaw the use of alcoholic drinks.
Greenback Party (1876) called for the increased circulation of paper money to help the nation prosper.
Populist Party (1891) worked to help farmers.
Socialist Party (1901) wanted greater public control of the nation's means of production.
Progressive Party (1912), also known as the Bull Moose Party, was an offshoot of the Republican Party and called for social and economic reform. Theodore Roosevelt was its unsuccessful presidential candidate.
Communist Party (1919) supported the cause of communism.
Dixiecrat Party (1948), or the States' Rights Democratic Party, broke away from the Democratic Party because of its pro–civil rights platform.

POLITICAL PARTIES

A political party is an organized group of individuals whose goal is to obtain political power. In some countries, especially dictatorships, there is only one party. In other countries there may be many different political parties. This multiparty system is common in many countries of Western Europe, Asia, and Latin America.

The United States has a two-party system. There are two major political parties, the DEMOCRATIC PARTY and the REPUBLICAN PARTY. These parties compete in national, state, and local elections. Every four years they hold national conventions to choose their presidential and vice presidential candidates.

The FEDERALIST Party was the first U.S. political party. Federalists wanted a strong central government. This party began to form in 1787, even before George Washington became the country's first president. The Federalists were opposed by the Democratic-Republicans, who wanted a weak central government. In the 1820s, the Democratic-Republicans, led by Andrew JACKSON, changed the name of their party to the Democratic Party. The Republican Party was formed in 1854 as an anti-slavery party.

Throughout its history, the United States has had many "third parties." But none of these has ever been strong enough to win a presidential election.

The two major political parties in Canada are the Progressive Conservative Party and the Liberal Party.

► *George Bush and Dan Quayle were nominated as candidates for president and vice president at the 1988 Republican National Convention in New Orleans, Louisiana. Each party has a convention to choose candidates and to approve ideas for the campaigns.*

POLK, James K.

James Knox Polk was the 11th president of the United States. During Polk's presidency, California and much of the Southwest became part of the United States.

Polk, a lawyer, was elected to the U.S. House of Representatives from Tennessee in 1835. He served there until 1839, when he was elected governor of the state. In 1844, Polk won the Democratic presidential nomination and went on to defeat Henry CLAY in the presidential election.

Polk was one of the strongest presidents of the 19th century. He believed in MANIFEST DESTINY—the right of the United States to expand westward across the continent. He demanded—and got—the annexation of Texas. He also urged Congress to declare war on Mexico. As a result of the MEXICAN WAR (1846–1848),

▲ Under President Polk, the United States defeated Mexico in a war over territory.

the United States acquired what are now California, Nevada, Utah, and parts of Arizona, New Mexico, Colorado, and Wyoming. Polk also settled a controversy with Britain over the Oregon Territory. The two countries agreed to set the northern boundary of Oregon at the 49th parallel.

Polk was very skillful at influencing Congress, and he was able to achieve two other important goals. He reduced the tariff—tax on goods brought into the country. And he re-established an independent treasury.

Polk was the first president not to seek re-election. His four years in office had exhausted him, and he died three months after leaving office.

James Knox Polk
Born: November 2, 1795, near Pineville, North Carolina
Education: University of North Carolina
Political party: Democratic
Term of office: 1845–1849
Married: 1824 to Sarah Childress
Died: June 15, 1849, in Nashville, Tennessee

Pollutants may be carried by the wind from one country to another, sometimes over a distance of thousands of miles. Lakes in eastern Canada have been poisoned by acid rain that originated in the United States.

POLLUTION

Pollution is the discharge of harmful materials into the environment. There are three main kinds of pollution—air, soil, and water. Air pollution is caused by the discharge of certain gases into the air. The burning of coal to run factories and produce electricity and the burning of gasoline to power cars and trucks causes air pollution. Besides harming health, air pollution causes acid rain in which rain and snow carry toxic chemicals. Pollution from one country can travel hundreds of miles to create acid rain in a neighboring country.

Soil and water pollution are caused mostly by manufacturing plants and farming. Harmful chemicals and fertilizers get into the ground, as well as rivers, lakes, and the ocean. This contaminates drinking water and kills birds and other animals. Fish become contaminated, and this can be harmful to the people who eat them. Waste is another major pollution problem.

The Environmental Protection Agency, a governmental agency, leads the fight to control pollution.

▶ Chemical factories line the waterfront at Tacoma, Washington. Air and water pollution are still hazards, despite federal, state, and local laws to protect the environment.

▼ Ponce de León failed to discover a fountain of youth, but his exploration led to Spanish settlement of Florida.

PONCE DE LEÓN, Juan

Juan Ponce de León (1460–1521) was the Spanish explorer who discovered Florida. He sailed with Christopher Columbus on his second voyage to the Americas in 1493. After defeating the Indians on the island of Hispaniola, he was made its governor. He soon began to seek the legendary "Fountain of Youth." This led him to the land he called Florida ("full of flowers"). In 1513 he became the first European to set foot there.

PONTIAC

Pontiac (1720?–1769) was an Ottawa Indian chief. During the FRENCH AND INDIAN WAR he fought alongside the French against the British. After France's defeat in 1763, the British began settling on Indian land. An angry Pontiac led the Ottawas and other Algonquian tribes in what is known as Pontiac's Rebellion, or Conspiracy. They attacked and captured nine British forts in the Great Lakes region. Only Detroit and Fort Pitt in Pennsylvania held out. The Indians were finally defeated in 1765. Pontiac then helped the British defeat bands of Indians who had not given up. This caused great hostility, and a Peoria Indian assassinated Pontiac.

▲ In 1763, Pontiac picked up the war hatchet to begin the Ottawa Indian struggle to drive out the British. He told an Indian gathering: "We must exterminate from our land the nation whose only object is our death."

PONY EXPRESS

The pony express was a system of delivering mail by horseback. It operated between St. Joseph, Missouri, and Sacramento, California, from April 1860 to October 1861. It used relays of riders—about 80 in all—and 400 horses, which were kept in readiness at the 157 stations along the 2,000-mile (3,200-km) route. When a rider reached a station he dismounted, changed to a fresh horse, and continued on his way.

The opening of the transcontinental telegraph service in October 1861 made the pony express unnecessary, and it closed down.

▼ Teams of pony express riders could carry mail from St. Joseph, Missouri, to Sacramento, California, in ten days. That was less than half the time mail took by stagecoach.

▶ *Diana Ross has remained popular during the many changes in the world of popular music.*

▼ *Stephen Foster wrote some of America's best-loved songs. Tunes such as "Oh! Susanna!" have become part of American culture.*

▼ *Nat King Cole was a respected jazz pianist who became even more famous as a singer. In the 1950s he became the first black person to host his own television program.*

POPULAR MUSIC

Many kinds of music are considered popular music. ROCK MUSIC, JAZZ, and music for musical comedies are forms of popular music. Popular music is distinct from classical, or serious, music, such as music for symphony orchestras, operas, and ballet.

Popular music in the United States is as old as the country itself. "Yankee Doodle," for example, dates from the time of the American Revolution. During the Civil War, Julia Ward HOWE's "Battle Hymn of the Republic" was the most popular song in the North. "Dixie" was the favorite tune in the South. Love was—and is—another major theme of popular songs. "Let Me Call You Sweetheart" was but one example from the early 1900s. New types of popular music began around this time, such as the blues. W. C. HANDY's "St. Louis Blues" is still popular. The blues were important in the development of jazz.

Popular music reached new heights of popularity in the 1920s and 1930s. This was brought about by radio, motion pictures, and sound recordings. Al JOLSON, Kate Smith, Bing Crosby, and other singers became celebrities. After World War II, Frank SINATRA, Nat King Cole, Dinah Shore, and Peggy Lee were among those who sang to America.

The world of popular music changed dramatically in the 1950s. Rock and roll was born. Elvis Presley and the Beatles from England sang a form of popular music that appealed especially to young people. Rock is still the dominant form of popular music.

PORCUPINE

The porcupine is a RODENT. The North American porcupine can weigh as much as 40 pounds (18 kg). Porcupines live in burrows or hollow trees in wooded areas. They travel about at night, searching for plants to eat. During the winter especially, porcupines will peel the bark off trees to eat the tender tissue underneath. Porcupines are covered with long, sharp quills. These serve as protection.

PORTER, Cole

Cole Porter (1892–1964) was one of the most gifted songwriters of the 20th century. He wrote not only the music of his songs but also the lyrics, which are witty and sophisticated. Among his best-known songs are "I Love Paris," "Night and Day," "Begin the Beguine," and "Anything Goes."

Porter was born into a wealthy family and began studying music as a child. At the age of ten he composed an operetta. His first Broadway hit show, *Fifty Million Frenchmen*, was followed by many other successes, including *Kiss Me Kate*, based on Shakespeare's *The Taming of the Shrew*. He also wrote songs for films.

PORTLAND

Portland is the largest city in OREGON. Located on the Williamette River near where it meets the Columbia River, Portland is the most important port in the Northwest. About 110 miles (177 km) from the Pacific Ocean, its docks can handle oceangoing ships. Portland's factories produce wood products, processed

▲ *A porcupine's quills are its best defense. They fan out when the porcupine is threatened. Some porcupines have as many as 30,000 quills.*

▲ *Cole Porter wrote some of the wittiest songs of the 1930s and 1940s. Many of his songs were for musical comedies.*

◄ *Portland is a busy American city and an important port. Portland also has 148 parks, including Forest Park, which covers 6,000 acres (2,400 ha).*

foods, and metal products, among other goods.

Portland was founded in 1845 and named for Portland, Maine. It grew rapidly during World War II, when shipbuilding yards were built there. Today the city has a population of about 437,000, and its mild climate continues to draw many settlers.

Busiest Ports and Harbors in the United States (by tons of cargo)
1. New Orleans, Louisiana
2. New York, New York
3. Houston, Texas
4. Valdez Harbor, Alaska
5. Baton Rouge, Louisiana
6. Corpus Christi, Texas
7. Long Beach, California
8. Tampa Harbor, Florida
9. Los Angeles, California
10. Norfolk Harbor, Virginia

▼ *The port of Houston is the processing and transport center of the important Texas oil industry. It is the third busiest U.S. port, handling more than 112 million tons of cargo each year.*

PORTS AND HARBORS

The first American cities in Colonial times were ports built around natural harbors. Boston, New York, and Charleston, South Carolina, all have deep natural harbors. Philadelphia, a river port on the Delaware River, is linked to the Atlantic Ocean by way of Delaware Bay. Over the past 200 years the importance of these eastern ports has declined, except for New York. As the U.S. population has shifted westward and southward, ports in the South, Midwest, and West have become busier. Freshwater ports along the Great Lakes—Buffalo, Chicago, and Detroit—were some of the first to rival the old Atlantic ports. Busy Gulf of Mexico ports include Galveston, Texas; New Orleans, Louisiana; Mobile, Alabama; and Tampa, Florida.

Each year more than $250 billion worth of goods arrive at U.S. ports. About $103 billion worth are

shipped as exports. Experts predict that in the next century Asian and Pacific nations will become more important trading partners than European nations. This should signal even more growth in West Coast ports such as Los Angeles and Long Beach, California; Portland, Oregon; Seattle, Washington; and Anchorage, Alaska.

A New England postal clerk in the early 1800s once had to forward a letter with the address:
**HILL
JOHN
MASS**
It took him only a few moments to realize that the letter should go to John Underhill, Andover, Massachusetts.

Stamps, passport applications, and other services

STAMPS PARCELS

Airmail

Sorting office

◄ *The U.S. Postal Service handles about 155 billion pieces of mail each year.*

Post office

City delivery

Rural delivery

Special delivery

POSTAL SERVICE

The U.S. Postal Service is an agency of the United States government. It operates the largest postal system in the world. It has 800,000 employees working in more than 30,000 post offices.

The Continental Congress created the first U.S. postal service in 1775. Benjamin Franklin was the first postmaster general. In 1789, Congress gave the federal government complete control of the postal system. U.S. postal stamps were first issued in 1847. In 1860 the PONY EXPRESS began carrying mail from Missouri to California. It ended the following year, however, when a coast-to-coast telegraph system was established. Soon trains began carrying the mail, and in this century airplanes have taken on much of the work.

Notable Dates in U.S. Postal Service History
1639 First official postal system established in Boston.
1775 Benjamin Franklin becomes the first postmaster general.
1789 Congress creates the U.S. Post Office Department.
1847 First postage stamps issued.
1860–61 The pony express service operates between Missouri and California. It became a popular way of mail transport.
1918 The first regular airmail route is established between Washington, D.C., and New York City.
1939 First transatlantic airmail flight.
1943 Major cities divided into numbered postal zones.
1963 ZIP (Zoning Improvement) codes introduced.
1971 The U.S. Postal Service replaces the U.S. Post Office Department.

Leading Potato-Producing States (1,000 *cwt/year)	
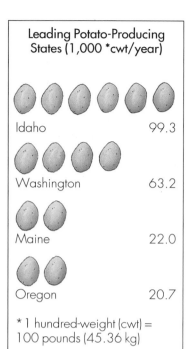
Idaho	99.3
Washington	63.2
Maine	22.0
Oregon	20.7

* 1 hundred-weight (cwt) = 100 pounds (45.36 kg)

POTATO

The potato is one of the world's main food crops, and the United States is one of the leading producers. Idaho is the principal potato-growing state, followed by Washington, Maine, Oregon, North Dakota, California, Wisconsin, and Colorado. The most popular varieties are the Russet Burbank, Norchip, Kennebec, and Katahdin. These account for more than two thirds of all the potatoes grown in the United States. Most are processed into french fries and potato chips.

Spanish explorers discovered the potato in Peru in the 1500s. It was an important part of the diet of the Incas. The Spanish took the potato to Europe. Immigration later brought it to the English colonies in North America, where it was first grown in the early 1700s.

POUND, Ezra

Ezra Pound (1885–1972) was one of the most important and controversial figures in modern literature. Born in Hailey, Ohio, he moved to Europe when he was in his early twenties. He edited poetry magazines and helped many younger writers, including Frost and Ernest Hemingway. His own poetry included *Cantos*, an epic poem that traced the growth of civilization.

Pound was disillusioned with the American way of life. During World War II he made pro-Fascist radio broadcasts from Italy. He was captured by American troops after the war and sent to the United States. He was tried for treason but judged to be insane and sent to an asylum. He was released after 12 years and then returned to Italy.

▼ *Adam Clayton Powell retained the loyalty of his constituents in Harlem though he was not always popular among fellow congressmen.*

POWELL, Adam Clayton, Jr.

Adam Clayton Powell, Jr. (1908–1972), was a congressman from Harlem in New York City. He was born in New Haven, Connecticut. In 1936, Powell became pastor of the Abyssinian Baptist Church in New York. He began to speak out against racism, and this led to his going into politics. In 1944, he entered the House of Representatives. Powell was always popular with the voters, but in the late 1960s, congressmen accused him of dishonesty and betraying public trust. He left politics in 1970.

POWELL, Colin L.

Colin L. Powell (1937–) was the first black and the youngest U.S. Army officer to become chairman of the Joint Chiefs of Staff, the group that oversees all U.S. military matters. Born in New York City, Powell entered the Army in 1958. He was wounded in combat during the Vietnam War and later held increasingly important commands. He also served as President Ronald Reagan's national security adviser. Powell was promoted to the rank of four-star general in January 1989 and became the head of the Joint Chiefs in August of that year.

POWHATAN

Powhatan (?–1618) was the name that English settlers at Jamestown, Virginia, gave to the Indian chief Wahunsonaock. He was the head of a group of tribes called the Powhatan Confederacy. His daughter, POCAHONTAS, married the English colonist John Rolfe. Powhatan and the English colonists lived together in peace. But four years after his death a war broke out.

PRAIRIE

A prairie is an area of flat or rolling grassland. The world's largest prairie is in central North America. At one time the prairie was covered with wild grasses, but

▲ General Colin L. Powell became chairman of the Joint Chiefs of Staff in 1989. Only the president, as commander in chief, is his military superior.

▼ Contour farming, seen here in Nebraska, means planting crops in varying levels along the rolling prairies.

most of it has now been turned into farmland or grazing land. Hot summers, cold winters, moderate rainfall, and rich soil characterize the prairie.

In the eastern part of the North American prairie, which receives the most rainfall, tall grasses grow naturally, and corn is the principal crop. West of this are the GREAT PLAINS, a dry area of short bunchgrass, mostly used for grazing. Between the two regions is the mixed-grass prairie, where wheat is the main crop.

PRAIRIE DOG

The prairie dog is a type of GROUND SQUIRREL. It lives in burrows in the ground, in large groups known as colonies or "towns." Gentle and sociable, prairie dogs groom one another and appear to kiss. If an enemy such as a COYOTE or RATTLESNAKE approaches, the prairie dogs will warn the others in the colony with their loud, sharp, barking call.

The animals are up to about 17 inches (43 cm) long, including the tail, and weigh about 1 to 2 pounds (0.5 to 1.0 kg). There are two main types. The black-tailed prairie dog is found in the GREAT PLAINS. The white-tailed prairie dog lives at higher elevations, from southern Montana to northern Arizona and New Mexico.

Prairie dogs were once very common, but ranchers regard them as pests and have poisoned large numbers of them. This has reduced not only the number of prairie dogs but also the animals who prey on them (such as the black-footed ferret, which is now threatened with extinction, and the burrowing owl).

▼ *The holes leading to the burrows of black-tailed prairie dogs are surrounded by mounds of earth to prevent the burrows from flooding. The prairie dogs maintain the mounds very carefully.*

PREHISTORIC ANIMALS

Prehistoric animals are those that lived more than 5,000 years ago. Many animal fossils (preserved remains) have been found in North America, particularly in Texas, New Mexico, Kansas, Utah, Arizona, Wyoming, and Colorado. Some are hundreds of millions of years old.

Many prehistoric animals were similar to today's animals; others were very different. The first animals with backbones to live on land were AMPHIBIANS. REPTILES evolved from them, with DINOSAURS dominating the world for 140 million years. The first INSECTS and BIRDS appeared at about the same time.

When the dinosaurs disappeared, mammals began to rule the earth. The first HORSE, Hyracotherium, and, later, the ancestors of the camel, lived in North America. Still later, Brontotheres, which looked rather like rhinoceroses, ranged across the continent. After that, saber-toothed tigers and bear-dogs appeared. Ancestors of the PRONGHORN and then ancestors of PIGS, SHEEP, and cattle grazed in the grasslands. Mastodons and mammoths (early elephants) were relatively recent—they died out "only" about 10,000 years ago.

PRESBYTERIANS

Presbyterians follow a form of PROTESTANTISM. Their religious practices had their beginnings in the teaching of John Calvin. He was a religious reformer during the Protestant Reformation of the 1500s. Presbyterians

▲ Remains of many prehistoric mammals were found in Los Angeles's famous La Brea tar pits. The animals—including the saber-toothed tiger, ground sloth, mastodon, and mammoth—had been trapped in the tar as they attempted to drink the rainwater underneath.

Scientists still cannot agree on the reason the most famous prehistoric animals, the dinosaurs, died out. Some say that a huge meteor crashed into the earth, throwing up dust that choked the dinosaurs. Others say they died out more slowly, as a result of gradual climate change.

The Presbyterian Church (U.S.A.) has more than 3 million members and about 12,000 congregations. The congregations are organized into larger groups called presbyteries, and the presbyteries into still larger units called synods.

Many people consider the president of the United States to be the most powerful elected leader in the world. As chief executive, the president is responsible for enforcing federal laws, developing national policies, preparing the budget, and appointing federal officials. As chief of state, he attends many ceremonial occasions. As commander in chief of the armed forces, he is responsible for the country's defense. He is also in charge of foreign policy.

▼ *The Seal of the President of the United States is a symbol of the nation's highest office.*

▶ *The president's daily duties are carried out in the Oval Office of the White House. Special advisers go there to keep the president informed about national and international events.*

practice a simple form of worship. They consider the Bible to be the final authority in matters of religion. Their services are conducted by elders, or presbyters. In non-English-speaking countries, Presbyterian churches are known as Reformed churches. The largest Presbyterian group in the United States is the Presbyterian Church (U.S.A.), with 3.3 million members.

PRESIDENT OF THE UNITED STATES

According to Article II of the CONSTITUTION of the United States, "The executive power shall be vested in a president of the United States of America." In the 200 years since the founding of the nation, there have been 40 presidents.

The president must be a natural-born citizen of the United States, at least 35 years old, and a resident of the United States for at least 14 years. Presidents are elected for a four-year term. Franklin D. ROOSEVELT, who was elected four times, was the longest-serving president (1933–1945). The Twenty-second Amendment to the Constitution (1951) provided that no one could be elected to the office more than twice.

The president is the head of state, the chief executive officer of the government, and the commander in chief of the armed forces. In carrying out his duties, he is advised by his CABINET. If the president dies in office, the vice president becomes president.

*Presidents and Vice Presidents of the United States

President	Party	Served	Vice President
George Washington (1732–1799)	None	1789–1797	John Adams
John Adams (1735–1826)	Federalist	1797–1801	Thomas Jefferson
Thomas Jefferson (1743–1826)	Democratic-Republican	1801–1809	Aaron Burr / George Clinton
James Madison (1751–1836)	Democratic-Republican	1809–1817	George Clinton / Elbridge Gerry
James Monroe (1758–1831)	Democratic-Republican	1817–1825	Daniel Tompkins
John Quincy Adams (1767–1848)	Democratic-Republican	1825–1829	John Calhoun
Andrew Jackson (1767–1845)	Democratic	1829–1837	John Calhoun / Martin Van Buren
Martin Van Buren (1782–1862)	Democratic	1837–1841	Richard Johnson
William H. Harrison (1773–1841)	Whig	1841	John Tyler
John Tyler (1790–1862)	Whig	1841–1845	
James K. Polk (1795–1849)	Democratic	1845–1849	George Dallas
Zachary Taylor (1784–1850)	Whig	1849–1850	Millard Fillmore
Millard Fillmore (1800–1874)	Whig	1850–1853	
Franklin Pierce (1804–1869)	Democratic	1853–1857	William King
James Buchanan (1791–1868)	Democratic	1857–1861	John Breckinridge
Abraham Lincoln (1809–1865)	Republican	1861–1865	Hannibal Hamlin / Andrew Johnson
Andrew Johnson (1808–1875)	Natl. Union	1865–1869	
Ulysses S. Grant (1822–1885)	Republican	1869–1877	Schuyler Colfax / Henry Wilson
Rutherford Hayes (1822–1893)	Republican	1877–1881	William Wheeler
James Garfield (1831–1881)	Republican	1881	Chester Arthur
Chester Arthur (1829–1886)	Republican	1881–1885	
Grover Cleveland (1837–1908)	Democratic	1885–1889	Thomas Hendricks
Benjamin Harrison (1833–1901)	Republican	1889–1893	Levi Morton
Grover Cleveland (1837–1908)	Democratic	1893–1897	Adlai Stevenson
William McKinley (1843–1901)	Republican	1897–1901	Garret Hobart / Theodore Roosevelt
Theodore Roosevelt (1858–1919)	Republican	1901–1909	Charles Fairbanks
William Taft (1857–1930)	Republican	1909–1913	James Sherman
Woodrow Wilson (1856–1924)	Democratic	1913–1921	Thomas Marshall
Warren Harding (1865–1923)	Republican	1921–1923	Calvin Coolidge
Calvin Coolidge (1872–1933)	Republican	1923–1929	Charles Dawes
Herbert Hoover (1874–1964)	Republican	1929–1933	Charles Curtis
Franklin D. Roosevelt (1882–1945)	Democratic	1933–1945	John Garner / Henry Wallace / Harry Truman
Harry Truman (1884–1972)	Democratic	1945–1953	Alben Barkley
Dwight Eisenhower (1890–1969)	Republican	1953–1961	Richard Nixon
John Kennedy (1917–1963)	Democratic	1961–1963	Lyndon Johnson
Lyndon Johnson (1908–1973)	Democratic	1963–1969	Hubert Humphrey
Richard Nixon (1913–)	Republican	1969–1974	Spiro Agnew / Gerald Ford
Gerald Ford (1913–)	Republican	1974–1977	Nelson Rockefeller
Jimmy Carter (1924–)	Democratic	1977–1981	Walter Mondale
Ronald Reagan (1911–)	Republican	1981–1989	George Bush
George Bush (1924–)	Republican	1989–	Dan Quayle

*A biography of every president appears in this encyclopedia.

▲ *Lester B. Pearson, Canadian prime minister from 1963 to 1968, received the 1957 Nobel Peace Prize.*

▼ *Brian Mulroney, of the Progressive Conservative Party, has been Canada's prime minister since 1984. He is fluent in Canada's two official languages, English and French.*

PRIME MINISTER OF CANADA

The prime minister of Canada is the head of the Canadian GOVERNMENT, but the reigning British monarch is the Canadian head of state. This system differs from that of the United States, where the president is the head of government and state. Canada has a parliamentary system of government. Every political party has a leader to represent it in the House of Commons, the lower house of the Canadian Parliament. If a party has a majority of seats in this house, its leader automatically becomes prime minister. Most Canadian prime ministers have come from either the Liberal Party or Progressive Conservative Party. Brian Mulroney, prime minister since 1984, is a Progressive Conservative. The first Canadian prime minister was Sir John A. MACDONALD, who had been one of the founders of independent Canada. The Canadian prime minister lives in an official residence maintained by the government in the Canadian capital of OTTAWA.

Prime Ministers of Canada		
Name	**Served**	**Political Party**
Sir John A. Macdonald	1867–1873	Conservative
Alexander Mackenzie	1873–1878	Liberal
Sir John A. Macdonald	1878–1891	Conservative
Sir John Abbott	1891–1892	Conservative
Sir John Thompson	1892–1894	Conservative
Sir Mackenzie Bowell	1894–1896	Conservative
Sir Charles Tupper	1896	Conservative
Sir Wilfred Laurier	1896–1911	Liberal
Sir Robert Borden	1911–1917	Conservative
Sir Robert Borden	1917–1920	Unionist
Arthur Meighen	1920–1921	Unionist
W. L. Mackenzie King	1921–1926	Liberal
Arthur Meighen	1926	Conservative
W. L. Mackenzie King	1926–1930	Liberal
Richard Bennett	1930–1935	Conservative
W. L. Mackenzie King	1935–1948	Liberal
Louis St. Laurent	1948–1957	Liberal
John Diefenbaker	1957–1963	Progressive Conservative
Lester B. Pearson	1963–1968	Liberal
Pierre E. Trudeau	1968–1979	Liberal
Charles Joseph Clark	1979–1980	Progressive Conservative
Pierre E. Trudeau	1980–1984	Liberal
John Turner	1984	Liberal
Brian Mulroney	1984–	Progressive Conservative

PRINCE EDWARD ISLAND

Prince Edward Island is the smallest Canadian province. It is one of Canada's four Atlantic provinces and the only province that is an island. It was discovered in 1534 by the French explorer Jacques CARTIER and claimed for France in 1603 by Samuel de CHAMPLAIN. In 1763, following the French and Indian War, it became British along with most of present-day Canada. For six years it was part of neighboring Nova Scotia, but in 1769 it became the Colony of St. John's Island. Its name was changed to Prince Edward Island in 1799.

Prince Edward Island, or "P.E.I." as it is known locally, lies in the Gulf of St. Lawrence. Farming and fishing are the principal industries. Warm currents keep the climate relatively mild. The waters around Prince Edward Island are said to be warmer than any on the east coast of North America north of Virginia. Uncrowded, sandy beaches and the promise of excellent seafood (particularly lobster) attract thousands of tourists each year.

▲ *Prince Edward Island's population lives mainly on farms. Potatoes are the province's most important crop.*

Lady's slipper

Prince Edward Island
Capital: Charlottetown
Area: 2,185 sq mi (5,660 km²). Rank: 10th
Population: 126,646 (1986). Rank: 10th
Entry into Confederation: July 1, 1873 (7th province)
Highest point: Queens County, 465 ft (125 m)

▶ Revenue agents display cases of liquor recovered after a raid on a speakeasy (secret barroom) in Washington, D.C., during Prohibition.

Prohibition was sometimes called the Noble Experiment by its supporters. It began in 1919, shortly after World War I had ended. The end of the war had caused many people to look for dramatic measures to improve life and guarantee peace. The experiment of banning alcohol was one such action.

▼ The pronghorn is about 3 feet (90 cm) tall at the shoulder. It can run at 44 miles per hour (70 km/hr), so that it usually escapes from wolves and coyotes.

PROHIBITION

Prohibition is the legal forbidding of the manufacture, sale, and transportation of alcoholic beverages. In the late 1800s and early 1900s, the Women's Christian Temperance Union (WCTU) and other groups fought for prohibition. They argued that alcohol is a dangerous drug that destroys family life and leads to crime.

Their efforts led to the Eighteenth Amendment to the U.S. Constitution, which went into effect in 1920. It banned the manufacture, sale, and transportation of alcoholic beverages in the United States. The Volstead Act of 1920 provided for the enforcement of prohibition. But enforcement was difficult. Gangsters set up illegal saloons called speakeasies, where they sold bootleg, or illegal, liquor. Gang warfare also became commonplace. When it was realized that the enforcement of prohibition would not work, the Twenty-first Amendment was passed. The Eighteenth Amendment was repealed, and prohibition ended.

PRONGHORN

The pronghorn is one of North America's fastest mammals. It is often called the American antelope, but it is not a true antelope. It is a unique animal with no close relatives. Both the male and female have unusual horns with two prongs. Bands of pronghorns live in open grassland, gathering into larger herds in the winter. At one time they were found all over the central and western United States, but they were hunted so much that their numbers dwindled. The pronghorn is now protected by law.

PROTESTANTISM

Protestantism is a form of CHRISTIANITY. Protestants generally trace their origins back to the Reformation, the religious reform movement that began in the Roman Catholic Church in Europe in the early 1500s. Many of the early Protestants came to the New World seeking the freedom to worship in their own way. Some churches, such as the Church of Jesus Christ of Latter-day Saints (Mormons), began in the United States itself. There are about 80 million Protestants in the United States. The Baptists are the largest group, with about 28.5 million members. Other groups include the Methodist (about 13.5 million), Lutheran (8.5 million), Pentecostal (almost 8 million), and Reformed (almost 8 million). The Episcopal Church (2.5 million) is part of the large worldwide Anglican Communion.

Leading Protestant Churches in the United States (millions of members)
1. Southern Baptist Convention (14.72)
2. United Methodist Church (9.12)
3. National Baptist Convention, U.S.A. (5.5)
4. Evangelical Lutheran Church in America (5.29)
5. Church of Jesus Christ of Latter–day Saints (4.00)
6. Presbyterian Church (U.S.A.) (3.3)
7. National Baptist Convention of America (2.67)
8. Lutheran Church – Missouri Synod (2.61)
9. Episcopal Church in the U.S.A. (2.46)
10. African Methodist Episcopal Church (2.21)

◀ The Congregational Church in South Newfane, Vermont, is typical of many Protestant churches in New England. Its simple design reflects the plain faith of the worshipers.

PUBLIC HEALTH

Public health is the organized community effort to protect the health of the members of the community. The provision of clean water, nutritional food, and proper sanitation is an important aspect of public health. Public health services also formulate laws regarding health. They set up programs to prevent or control diseases. These services also provide health care for the needy.

In the United States, there are local, state, and national public health services. State and local governments are the main public health providers. The United States government is involved primarily through the U.S. Public Health Service, a division of the Department of Health and Human Services. The most important international group is the World Health Organization (WHO), an agency of the United Nations.

▶ *Young people join in a parade in Willcox, Arizona to promote D.A.R.E., an anti-drug project.*

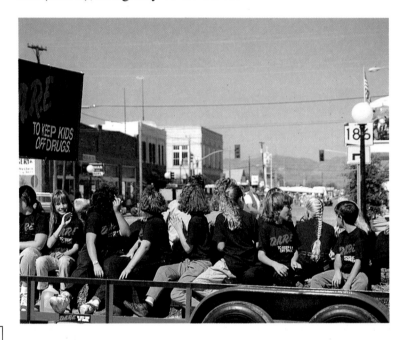

Top Public Utilities on the New York Stock Exchange

American Electric Power
Centerior Energy
Columbia Gas System
Commonwealth Edison
Consolidated Edison
Consolidated Natural Gas
Detroit Edison
Houston Industries
Niagara Mohawk Power
Pacific Gas & Electric
Panhandle Eastern
Peoples Energy
Philadelphia Electric
Public Service Enterprises
SCE

PUBLIC UTILITIES

A public utility is an industry that supplies certain essential services to the public. Such services include electricity, natural gas, water, garbage disposal, telephone and telegraph communication, and public transportation.

In most countries public utilities are owned by the government. In the United States they are regulated by the government rather than owned. One notable exception in the United States is the Tennessee Valley Authority (TVA), a hydroelectric system that is a government-owned corporation. And cities in the United States usually own and operate public transportation systems and water and sewer services.

▲ *Pueblo Indian women make and sell pottery at a backstreet stall. Pueblo pottery designs are more than 1,000 years old.*

PUEBLOS

The Pueblo INDIANS have lived in the Southwest for many centuries. Their homes are called *pueblos*, which means "town" in Spanish. Many of these homes look like multi-storied apartment buildings. Long ago the ancestors of the Pueblo Indians built their homes into cliffs, and they were known as CLIFF DWELLERS.

There are a number of groups of Pueblo Indians in Arizona and New Mexico, including the HOPI, Zuni, Tewa, Tiwa, Towa, and Keresan. Spanish explorers discovered them in the 1500s. They used them as forced labor and tried to destroy their ancient religion. This led to a number of revolts in the late 1500s and again in the late 1600s. The Pueblos also revolted against American rule in the late 1840s. There are more than 48,000 Pueblos today. They are known for their beautiful pottery, woven baskets, and silverwork.

The Spanish conquistador Francisco de Coronado was the first European to come across the Pueblo culture. During a mission in 1542 he sent a scout ahead to examine the Pueblo town of Acoma. The scout described the cliff-top settlement as "a great city in the sky...the strongest position ever seen in the world."

▼ *San Juan is the capital of Puerto Rico and its largest city. The city combines modern and historical architecture in a beautiful setting.*

PUERTO RICO

Puerto Rico is a self-governing part of the United States. It is a beautiful island in the Caribbean Sea, and tourism is important to its economy. Each year, about 1.5 million visitors enjoy its sandy beaches and pleasant climate. Agriculture is also important; sugarcane, coffee, and bananas are among the major crops. Puerto Rican factories turn out many products, including

▲ *Casimir Pulaski's cavalry leadership helped secure many American successes during the Revolutionary War.*

pharmaceuticals, chemicals, petroleum products, machinery, clothing, and textiles.

Christopher COLUMBUS discovered Puerto Rico in 1493. The first Spanish settlement was built there in 1508. It remained a Spanish colony until 1898, when the United States took control following the SPANISH-AMERICAN WAR. The island became a commonwealth in 1952. Today there are 3.3 million Puerto Ricans on the island. About half of them live in and around San Juan, the capital. Another 2 million Puerto Ricans live on the U.S. mainland. The Puerto Rican people continue to debate the status of their homeland. Many want Puerto Rico to remain a commonwealth associated with the United States. Others want it to become the 51st state. And still others want it to become independent.

PULASKI, Casimir

Casimir Pulaski (1747–1779) was a Polish patriot and soldier who helped the American colonists win their independence from Britain. Forced to leave Poland because of his part in armed rebellions against its Russian conquerors, Pulaski went to the colonies in 1777 and joined the Continental Army. In 1778 he formed Pulaski's Legion, a corps of cavalrymen and infantrymen. In May 1779, Pulaski's Legion prevented the British from capturing Charleston, South Carolina. Pulaski was fatally wounded during the siege of Savannah soon afterward.

PULITZER PRIZES

The Pulitzer Prizes are awarded each year for outstanding achievements in American journalism, literature, and music. The prizes were established in 1917, with funds left by the late newspaper editor Joseph Pulitzer (1847–1911). Pulitzer also left funds to establish a school of journalism at Columbia University.

The trustees of Columbia University make the awards. There are 14 prizes in journalism. They include prizes for local, national, and international reporting and editorial writing. Awards are also made for political cartoons and news photography. The literature awards are for fiction, drama, history, biography or autobiography, poetry, and general nonfiction. The music award, for composition, has been awarded since 1943.

▼ *Money that Joseph Pulitzer left to Columbia University in 1911 became the basis for the Pulitzer Prizes. Each year the university presents Pulitzer Prizes for 21 categories of journalism, writing, and music.*

PURITANS

The Puritans were originally members of the Church of England. But they believed in simple ways of worshiping and in a simple church organization. They did not like some of the church's elaborate ceremonies, music, or even the dress of the church officials. They wanted to purify the church of these things. Some Puritans—called Separatists—even left the church. One group of Separatists, known as the Pilgrims, founded PLYMOUTH COLONY in 1620.

Thousands of Puritans followed the Pilgrims to the New World. In 1630 they founded Massachusetts Bay Colony. As other colonies were founded, the Puritans came to dominate the political and cultural life in New England. At that time, church and state were not separate, as they are today. The Puritans allowed only church members to vote in the affairs of the Massachusetts Bay Colony. The Puritan administration abolished many traditional English holidays, such as May Day and St. Valentine's Day. They considered such holidays frivolous and not in keeping with the simple Puritan faith. Roger WILLIAMS, the founder of Rhode Island, was a Puritan. But he was forced out of Massachusetts because he attacked the Puritan leaders for not practicing religious toleration.

Puritanism was an important force in New England even into the 1800s.

The first Puritan settlers knew nothing about how to live in the wilderness that was America. They spent their first winter in sailcloth tents. Nearly a quarter of them died from hunger, exposure, and disease before a ship from England brought fresh supplies.

▼ Puritans faced many difficulties in their new country. Establishing settlements meant that land had to be cleared for building—even in the harsh New England winter.

QUAIL

North American quails are types of grouse. These game birds are popular with hunters, and they have been hunted so much that they are protected in many states. The best known is the bobwhite, or partridge, the only quail found east of the Mississippi River. The largest is the mountain, or plumed, quail. Mearns's quail, the smallest, is the only one that doesn't have a crest on its head. Other quails include the California, or valley, quail; scaled, or blue, quail; and Gambel's, or desert, quail.

▶ Quails are easy to identify because of their plume, neck, and small beak. They are a popular game bird, especially in the South.

QUAKERS See Friends, Society of

▼ Quanah Parker was chief of the Quahadi Comanches, the last band to surrender in the South Plains war of 1874–1875.

QUANAH PARKER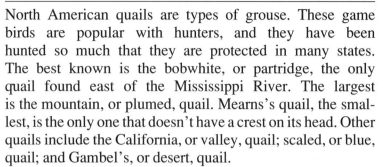

Quanah Parker (1845?–1911) was a COMANCHE Indian chief. His mother, Cynthia, was a white woman who had been captured by the Comanches as a child. She later married Nokoni, a Comanche chief. When Nokoni died, Quanah became chief. In the 1870s, white settlers continued to invade Indian lands, slaughtering the buffalo. In 1874, Quanah led a band of Comanches, Cheyennes, and Kiowas against the Adobe Walls fort in Texas. Quanah surrendered in 1875. He became an able businessman and encouraged his people to go to school.

Quebec is the largest province in Canada. It stretches from the St. Lawrence River in the south to Hudson Strait in the north. Much of northern Quebec is a forested wilderness. Most people live in the south, in such cities as MONTREAL and QUEBEC CITY, the capital. Quebec has more people than any other province except neighboring Ontario. The province is the center of French culture in Canada.

Jacques CARTIER claimed the Quebec region for France in 1534. Quebec City was founded in 1608 by Samuel de CHAMPLAIN. This was the start of the colony of NEW FRANCE. In 1763, however, after France was defeated by Britain in the FRENCH AND INDIAN WAR, it was forced to give up its North American colonies. Quebec joined the Canadian confederation in 1867. During the 1900s, some French Canadians have sought to separate their province from the rest of Canada. But in 1980 the people of Quebec voted against a plan to make their province politically independent.

Quebec's factories make automobiles, aircraft, machinery, chemical and petroleum products, food products, and many other kinds of goods. Its vast northern region is a treasure trove of minerals. Tourism and lumbering are other important industries.

▲ The church of St. Saveur nestles in the wooded foothills of the Laurentides of Quebec. Most French-speaking Quebecers belong to the Roman Catholic Church.

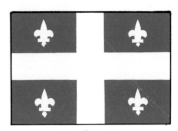

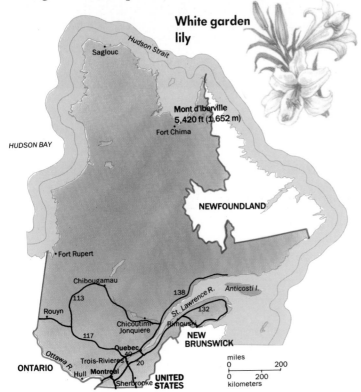

White garden lily

Quebec
Capital: Quebec City
Area: 594,860 sq mi (1,540,680 km²). Rank: 1st
Population: 6,540,276 (1986). Rank: 2nd
Entry into Confederation: July 1, 1867 (one of the first four provinces)
Highest point: Mont d'Iberville, 5,420 ft (1,652 m)

QUEBEC, Battle of

The Battle of Quebec was the most important battle of the FRENCH AND INDIAN WAR. The decisive British victory over French troops forced France to give up its American colonies.

QUEBEC CITY is located high above the St. Lawrence River. This position makes it difficult to attack. But on the night of September 12–13, 1759, the British general James WOLFE secretly landed 4,000 troops just west of the city on the Plains of Abraham. The French commander, the Marquis de Montcalm, did not expect an attack here, and the British won a decisive victory. Both Wolfe and Montcalm were killed in the battle.

▶ *This British print, based on eyewitness accounts, depicts the Battle of Quebec in 1759.*

QUEBEC ACT

The Quebec Act was passed by the British Parliament in 1774. It guaranteed the use of the French language in QUEBEC and recognized the Roman Catholic religion there. It also enlarged Quebec to include much of what is now the midwestern United States. The British passed this act in the hope that the French Canadians would help them or remain neutral if the 13 American colonies revolted.

In 1774 the British also passed what are known as the Intolerable Acts. These closed the port of Boston and forced the colonists to house and feed British soldiers. The colonists believed that the Quebec Act was just one more Intolerable Act. These acts helped unite the American colonies in their desire to end British rule.

◀ The Chateau Frontenac (background), a hotel built in the 1800s in the French style, stands on the highest point of Quebec City.

Quebec City was the scene of two important meetings between President Franklin D. Roosevelt and the British prime minister, Winston Churchill, during World War II. The first meeting, in 1943, discussed plans for the European offensive later known as D Day. The second, in 1944, planned war efforts in the Pacific Ocean.

QUEBEC CITY

Quebec City is the capital of the Canadian province of QUEBEC. It is located in the southern part of the province, on the northern bank of the St. Lawrence River. The city is the center of French Canada, and 96 percent of the people speak French.

Quebec City has two distinct areas, Upper Town and Lower Town. Upper Town is located on top of a cliff overlooking the St. Lawrence. Its business and residential areas are surrounded by stone walls that were built in the 1600s. This area has an Old World flavor. The Lower Town stretches along the river. This section is the city's business and industrial center.

Samuel de CHAMPLAIN founded Quebec City in 1608 as a fort and trading post. It is the oldest city in Canada. It became the capital of NEW FRANCE in 1663. The British captured the city in 1759 during the FRENCH AND INDIAN WAR. Today it is an important industrial center and one of Canada's most important ports.

▼ A view of Quebec City's harbor. The city's location on the St. Lawrence River makes it an important port.

▼ *Rabbits and their larger relatives, hares, use their coloring to blend into surroundings and escape from enemies.*

Snowshoe hare

Eastern cottontail

▲ *A raccoon's black "mask" and striped tail make it easy to identify in daylight. But raccoons are nocturnal and scavenge mainly at night.*

The American Indians hunted raccoons before the white people came. After the arrival of the settlers, they exchanged raccoon skins for guns and other items. The settlers also used raccoon furs as money before a currency was established.

RABBITS AND HARES

The wild rabbits found in North America are cottontails, or New World rabbits. They have fluffy tails that are white or light-colored on the underside. Cottontails usually live on open land. The eastern, or Florida, cottontail is the most common. It is found east of the Rocky Mountains, as well as in southeastern Canada and eastern Mexico. There are also desert, mountain, and New England cottontails.

The JACKRABBIT (which is a hare, not a rabbit) and the snowshoe hare are both North American hares.

RACCOON

A relative of the panda, the raccoon is up to 3 feet (90 cm) long, including the tail. The species known as the northern raccoon is found almost all over the United States and in parts of Canada and Central America.

The raccoon prefers to make its home in woods near water. A good climber, it usually sleeps in a den in a hollow tree or log. In areas with no trees, it may make its nest in tall grass or in an abandoned building. The raccoon sleeps by day and comes out at night to hunt for food. It eats crabs, crayfish, small animals, and fruit. The raccoon is widely hunted for its fur and meat.

RACHMANINOFF, Sergey

Sergey Rachmaninoff (1873–1943) was a Russian-born composer, pianist, and conductor. He wrote some of the most richly melodic music of the 20th century. In the year of his graduation from the Moscow Conservatory (1892) he produced one of his most popular compositions, the Prelude in C-Sharp Minor. His lushly romantic Second Piano Concerto was first performed in 1901.

Rachmaninoff settled in the United States in 1917. There, he had an active career as a concert pianist, while continuing to compose. The *Rhapsody on a Theme of Paganini* is a famous piece from this period.

RACIAL DISCRIMINATION *See* Civil Rights

RADIO BROADCASTING

There are about 9,000 radio stations in the United States. About 90 percent of them are commercial stations that broadcast music. These stations are regulated by the Federal Communications Commission. It assigns radio frequencies and approves the stations' call letters. The call letters of stations east of the Mississippi River begin with the letter W, as in WCBS. Those west of the Mississippi begin with the letter K.

Before television started in the early 1950s, the radio was the chief source of entertainment and news for most people. Regular radio broadcasting started about 1920. The period from 1920 until the 1940s was known as the Golden Age of Radio. People would sit for hours listening to such programs as "Gangbusters," "The Lone Ranger" and "Superman."

The power of radio at its peak became known on the night of October 30, 1938. The actor Orson Welles, then only 23 years old, broadcast a reading of the novel *War of the Worlds*, by H. G. Wells. Millions of people were swept into panic and confusion by the tale of Martians landing in New Jersey. Many Americans believed it was a real news broadcast. They never heard Welles admit that it was a Halloween spoof.

◄ *A disc jockey and a radio advertiser check a day's playlist. The playlist shows the music and advertising schedule.*

▶ *Railroad posters of the 1800s confidently predicted that trains would link some of the continents.*

Important Dates in
U.S. Railroad History
1831 The United States' first regular steam-powered railroad begins operating in South Carolina.
1859 George Pullman builds the first sleeping car.
1869 The Union Pacific and Central Pacific railroads complete the world's first transcontinental railroad line.
1887 The Interstate Commerce Commission is formed to regulate railroad rates.
1970 Amtrak is created to operate intercity passenger trains in the United States.

The completion of the transcontinental railroad line in 1869 led to a rise in daring, violent train robberies in the West. Gangs led by hardened criminals such as Jesse James and Sam Bass attacked trains carrying mail, gold, and bank deposits. In one train robbery in 1899, Butch Cassidy and his "Wild Bunch" made off with $60,000 in cash.

▶ *Train lines connect cities all across the United States. Train travel from the Atlantic Ocean to the Pacific has been possible since 1869.*

RAILROADS

The railroad is an important means of transportation. In the United States, railroads carry about 4 million passengers and 1.4 billion tons of freight each year.

At first, railroad cars were pulled along tracks by horses. Steam-powered LOCOMOTIVES were first used in England in 1825. The first American steam-powered railroad was built in South Carolina in 1831. By 1860 there were 30,000 miles (48,000 km) of track in the United States, and the United States and Canada were rushing to complete transcontinental railroad lines. The Union Pacific Railroad built its track west from Omaha, Nebraska. The Central Pacific Railroad built east from

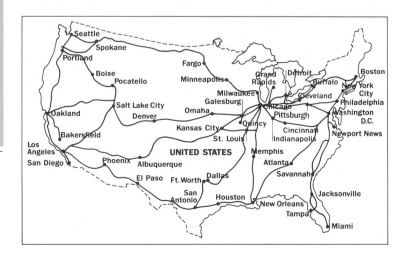

◄ A Southern locomotive flies the Confederate flag during the Civil War. Railroads played an important role in the war. The South's railroad network could not compete with the North's.

Sacramento, California. The two lines met in Promontory, Utah, in 1869. Sixteen years later the Canadian Pacific Railroad completed a line from Montreal, Quebec, to Vancouver, British Columbia. These rail lines opened the way for settlement of the American and Canadian west.

By 1916, United States railroads had 254,000 miles (406,000 km) of lines. But soon, automobiles, trucks, and airplanes began to compete with railroads for passenger and freight traffic. Railroads went into a decline. In 1970 the U.S. government was forced to take over the operation of most intercity railroads. It established the National Railroad Passenger Corporation (Amtrak) to operate the lines. Today, railroads carry almost as much freight as airlines, trucks, and barges combined. See also SUBWAYS.

▲ A freight train carries cargo through the wilderness of the United States.

◄ Trains carry passengers through the snowy Colorado landscape.

▲ *Sir Walter Raleigh's American explorations brought him great fame at home in England. He was one of the first people to suggest an English empire in America.*

▶ *Many modern ranchers still use the traditional cowboy skills of roping cattle with a lasso during a roundup.*

American ranch life has always centered around the cowboy, the hero of many movies, books, and songs. He first appeared in Texas around 1836, and soon ranches spread to almost every part of the West. Cowboys' lives centered on the cattle drive every spring and autumn when great herds were driven over vast areas to the nearest railroad terminal. During these drives the men were often on horseback for 15 hours a day.

RALEIGH, Sir Walter

Sir Walter Raleigh (1554?–1618) was an English writer, soldier, and explorer. He was among the first to try to establish an English colony in America.

Raleigh was a favorite of Queen Elizabeth I, and she made him a knight. In 1585, Raleigh sent a group of settlers to what is now North Carolina. They found life there too difficult and returned to England the following year. A second group of colonists, sent by Raleigh in 1588, disappeared, and their colony has become known as the LOST COLONY.

Raleigh fought bravely during England's wars with Spain in the late 1500s. When Queen Elizabeth died in 1603, James I, an enemy of Raleigh's, became king. He accused Raleigh of treason and kept him a prisoner in the Tower of London for 12 years. Raleigh was freed to search for gold in South America, but in 1618 James had him executed.

RANCHING

Ranching is the raising of cattle or other animals, such as sheep, on ranches, or large farms. In the United States there are about 95 million head of cattle. Most ranches are in the West and Southwest.

The first ranches were established in the mid-1800s. Cattle ranchers allowed their herds to graze on the wide-open ranges of the West. COWBOYS looked after the herds of cattle, protecting them from rustlers. They also drove the herds to railheads in Kansas and Nebraska. Here they were loaded aboard the trains for shipment to markets in the East.

Today ranches are much smaller than they were during the heyday of cattle ranching in the years after the Civil War. Jeeps and helicopters have largely replaced the legendary cowboys on horseback.

RANDOLPH, A. Philip

A. Philip Randolph (1889–1979) was an American labor leader. He played a major part in bringing black workers into the labor movement. Randolph first became interested in this cause while working his way through college in New York City. His efforts to organize black workers finally began to succeed in 1925, when he founded the Brotherhood of Sleeping Car Porters. At the beginning of World War II he prevailed on President Franklin D. Roosevelt to end discrimination against blacks in government jobs and in defense industries. Randolph also took an active part in the CIVIL RIGHTS movement of the 1960s.

▲ In the 1920s, A. Philip Randolph organized the first labor union representing black employees. He was still active in the civil rights movement of the 1960s.

RANKIN, Jeanette

Jeanette Rankin (1880–1973) was the first woman elected to the U.S. Congress. She was born in Montana and graduated from the University of Montana in 1902. She soon became a fighter for women's SUFFRAGE, the right of women to vote. In 1916, Rankin, a Republican, was elected to the U.S. House of Representatives from Montana. She served one term, during which she opposed U.S. entry into World War I. From 1918 to 1940, Rankin was a social worker. She became a Montana congresswoman again in 1941, serving until 1943. She cast the only congressional vote against U.S. entry into World War II.

▼ The Norway rat, sometimes called the house rat, is found around the world.

Norway rat

RAT

A rat is a RODENT (gnawing mammal). There are more than 100 types of rats in the world. The only two that live near people are the black rat and the brown, or Norway, rat. The brown rat is found all over the United States. It is larger—up to 10 inches (25 cm) long—and fiercer than the black rat and is a good swimmer. The white rat is a domesticated variety of brown rat. In the United States the black rat is found near ports. It is up to 8 inches (20 cm) long.

Rats live in large groups, making nests in or near buildings. They feed mostly at night and will eat practically any plant or animal. Rats can produce up to seven litters a year, each containing 6 to 22 young. They cause great damage, by destroying poultry, lambs, crops, and stored grain and by passing on many diseases.

▶ *The rattling of a rattlesnake's tail is a warning to stay away. Most rattlesnake bites are not fatal (deadly), but they are always painful.*

The Mojave rattlesnake is one of the deadliest snakes in North America. Its bite can paralyze a person's limbs or even cause death, unless the victim is treated quickly with antivenin, a drug made from the snake's poisonous venom.

▼ *Sam Rayburn had three terms as Speaker of the House of Representatives between 1940 and 1961. He held the position for 17 years, longer than anyone else in history.*

RATTLESNAKE

The rattlesnake is a poisonous SNAKE with a rattle on its tail. Often it gives a warning before it strikes, by lifting its tail and shaking the rattle, but some of the larger ones do not always rattle before biting.

Rattlesnakes are found from Canada to South America, generally in dry regions. The greatest number live in the southwestern United States and Mexico. The largest and most dangerous of the U.S. rattlesnakes are the diamondbacks. The eastern diamondback is up to 8 feet (2.5 m) long. The sidewinder is one of the smallest. About 18 inches (45 cm) long, it gets its name from the S-shaped curve it makes when moving across the desert.

RAYBURN, Sam

Sam Rayburn (1882–1961) was a member of the U.S. House of Representatives for almost 49 years. He was born in Roane County, Tennessee, but spent almost his whole life in Texas. Rayburn studied law at the University of Texas and was a lawyer for a short time. But he quickly became interested in politics, and in 1912 he was elected to the U.S. House of Representatives. He was re-elected 24 times. Rayburn held the powerful position of Speaker of the House for 17 years.

REAGAN, Ronald W.

Ronald Wilson Reagan was the 40th president of the United States. He served two terms, from 1981 to 1989, and was one of the most popular presidents in U.S. history.

Starting his career as a sports announcer, Reagan turned to acting in 1937. He appeared in more than 50 films. Originally a liberal, Reagan joined the Republican Party in 1962. Five years later he won the governorship of California. He served for eight years. In 1980 the Republican Party chose him as its presidential candidate. Reagan easily defeated Democrat Jimmy CARTER. Two months after his inauguration, Reagan was injured in an assassination attempt.

As president, Reagan reduced government spending on domestic programs, but he increased defense spending. And he maintained a strongly anti-Soviet and anti-

◄ Reagan is seen here accompanied by his vice president, George Bush, and Soviet leader Mikhail Gorbachev. Reagan's meetings with Gorbachev eased tensions between the United States and the USSR. In 1987 the two leaders signed a treaty that led to the reduction of nuclear arms.

Communist stand. He ordered U.S. troops to invade the Caribbean nation of Grenada in 1983 to oust a pro-Communist government. He supported guerrilla forces that opposed the Communist government in Nicaragua. He supplied weapons to rebel forces in Afghanistan that were fighting against the Soviet-backed government. And in 1986 he ordered U.S. planes to bomb Libya because that North African country supported terrorism. In 1987, however, Reagan and Soviet leader Mikhail Gorbachev signed a treaty eliminating short- and medium-range missiles from Europe.

In domestic affairs, Reagan's presidency was marked by increasing budget deficits and trade deficits. But the U.S. economy was strong during his eight years in office.

Ronald Reagan
Born: February 6, 1911, in Tampico, Illinois
Education: Eureka College
Political party: Republican
Term of office: 1981–1989
Married: 1940 to Jane Wyman (divorced 1948); 1952 to Nancy Davis

▲ The Reconstruction period after the Civil War gave many former slaves their first taste of education. This illustration from the period shows how young and old attended the same classes.

The Reconstruction Years
1865 War Department sets up Freedmen's Bureau to help freed slaves. Congress forms Committee on Reconstruction. Thirteenth Amendment bans slavery.
1866 Blacks granted citizenship. Ku Klux Klan spreads through the South; race riots in southern cities.
1867 Congress divides South into five regions and appoints military governors. "Carpetbaggers" arrive from the North.
1868 4th Reconstruction Act strengthens blacks' rights.
1877 Federal troops withdrawn from South.

RECONSTRUCTION

Reconstruction was the process of bringing the former CONFEDERATE STATES back into the Union after the CIVIL WAR. The Reconstruction period lasted from 1865 to 1877. President Andrew JOHNSON wanted to follow President Abraham LINCOLN's policy of dealing leniently with the South. He was opposed by Radical Republicans in Congress. They wanted the South dealt with harshly.

Three amendments to the U.S. Constitution were ratified during Reconstruction. The Thirteenth Amendment abolished slavery. The Fourteenth Amendment gave citizenship to former black slaves. And the Fifteenth Amendment gave blacks the right to vote. But the southern states did not want to give blacks equality. They passed the Black Codes to keep blacks "in their place." As a result, Congress passed the Reconstruction Acts of 1867. Federal troops were sent to the South, and new state governments were set up. They were run mainly by northerners (carpetbaggers), their southern collaborators (scalawags), and blacks. Some blacks also represented southern states in Congress.

By 1870, the southern states were re-admitted to the Union. But the KU KLUX KLAN terrorized and killed many blacks. After federal troops were withdrawn in 1877, southern whites regained control of their state governments. They established a system of segregation (racial separation) that lasted for almost a century.

RED CROSS

The American Red Cross is a voluntary relief organization. It is best known for providing help in times of disasters and emergencies. The Red Cross has a large blood donor program. It provides assistance for members of the armed forces and their families. And it gives courses in first aid, home nursing, water skills, parenting and child care, and home hygiene.

The American Red Cross is one of 126 national organizations that make up the international Red Cross, which was founded in 1863. The American Red Cross was founded in 1881 by Clara BARTON.

REED, Walter

The work of Dr. Walter Reed (1851–1902) led to the control of yellow fever, a deadly disease.

Born in Virginia, Reed studied medicine at the University of Virginia and at Bellevue Hospital Medical College in New York City. He joined the U.S. Army as a surgeon in 1875. In 1900, Reed was sent to Cuba to deal with an outbreak of yellow fever among American soldiers stationed in that country since the Spanish-American War. He determined that the disease was carried and spread by a certain mosquito. With that knowledge, soldiers were sent to kill the mosquitoes and destroy their breeding grounds. The disease was brought under control. The Walter Reed Army Medical Center near Washington, D.C., is named for him.

RELIGIONS

About 60 percent of people in the United States, almost 150 million, are members of a religious group. A large majority, some 94 percent (141 million people) belong to Christian churches. The largest group of non-Christians are Jews, with almost 4 percent of all religious worshipers (just under 6 million). Some 2.5 million people, or 1.7 percent, are Muslims. Finally there is a tiny number of Buddhists and other non-Christians.

▲ *Walter Reed's medical research helped scientists eliminate yellow fever from many parts of the world.*

▼ *Roman Catholics form the largest single religious group in the United States, but the combined Protestant total is larger. Four out of every ten Americans attend religious services at least once a week.*

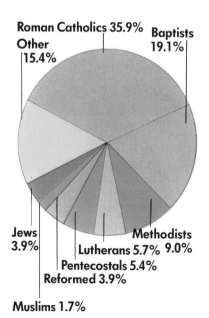

Roman Catholics 35.9%
Baptists 19.1%
Other 15.4%
Jews 3.9%
Methodists 9.0%
Lutherans 5.7%
Pentecostals 5.4%
Reformed 3.9%
Muslims 1.7%

619

▶ *The crocodile uses its powerful tail to swim and is recognizable by its long, pointed snout.*

▼ *Reptiles are cold-blooded and spend hours absorbing warmth from the sun. Special coloring and other devices, such as the turtle's shell, protect them from enemies.*

Green anole

Painted turtle

Eastern fence lizard

REPTILES

Reptiles are vertebrates—animals with backbones. They have dry, scaly skin and breathe air through their lungs. Reptiles found in the United States include LIZARDS, SNAKES, TURTLES, ALLIGATORS, and crocodiles. A reptile is cold-blooded—its body temperature changes with the temperature of its surroundings. For that reason there are more reptiles in the warmer parts of the United States, in particular the Southeast and the Southwest.

Most reptiles are harmless. Only a few are poisonous. The Gila monster is the only poisonous U.S. lizard. Poisonous snakes include the RATTLESNAKE, copperhead, and water moccasin. The alligator snapping turtle, one of the largest freshwater turtles, is not poisonous, but its massive, sharp jaws can wound a person. The largest U.S. reptile is the American crocodile, found on the coast of Florida. It is now an endangered species because, like many other reptiles, the crocodile was hunted for its skin.

REPUBLICAN PARTY

The Republican Party is one of two major POLITICAL PARTIES in the United States. Its symbol is the elephant. The nickname of the Republican Party is the G.O.P., or Grand Old Party.

The Republican Party was formed in 1854 as an antislavery party, but it soon broadened its appeal. The founders called themselves Republicicans because they favored national interests over states' rights. From their first victory in 1860, when Abraham LINCOLN won the presidency, the Republicans were in power for 56 of the next 72 years. In 1912 former president Theodore ROOSEVELT temporarily split the party when he formed the Progressive Party. The DEMOCRATIC PARTY won that election.

The Party was described as the "party of prosperity" during the 1920s. But as a result of the economic DEPRESSION that followed, the republicans lost the 1932 election to the Democrats. They did not regain control until 1952, when General Dwight EISENHOWER won the presidential election. The Republiicans were in power for 28 of the next 40 years.

The Republican Party was founded in 1854 by anti-slavery forces and Free Soil forces (a group founded in New York). In the congressional elections of that year, 44 Republicans were elected to the House of Representatives. They won control of the House in 1858. The Republicans ran their first presidential candidate, John C. Frémont, in 1856. He was defeated by James Buchanan.

REUTHER, Walter

Walter Reuther (1907–1970) was an important U.S. labor leader. Born in Wheeling, West Virginia, he organized a workers' protest when he was still a teen-ager. In 1935 he became president of a local chapter of the newly formed United Automobile Workers (UAW) union. He became UAW president in 1946, serving until his death in 1970. Reuther was also president of the Congress of Industrial Organizations (CIO) from 1952 to 1955, and a leader of the AFL-CIO from 1955 to 1968. During his career, Reuther fought for higher wages and better working conditions for workers. He also fought against union corruption.

REVERE, Paul

Paul Revere (1735–1818) was a patriot and hero of the American Revolution. He is most famous for his ride on horseback on April 18, 1775, to warn the MINUTEMEN of Lexington and Concord, Massachusetts, that the British were coming. Henry Wadsworth LONGFELLOW wrote a poem about this feat, called "Paul Revere's Ride."

Revere was born in Boston. Like his father, he was a silversmith. His copperplate engraving of the BOSTON MASSACRE helped to stir up patriotic anger against the British. Revere took part in the BOSTON TEA PARTY and was a leader of the SONS OF LIBERTY. During the war, he served as a lieutenant colonel.

Revere prospered after the war. He set up a mill for the manufacture of sheet copper, some of which was used on the hull of the U.S.S. CONSTITUTION. He also continued to design silver.

▼ *Paul Revere knew that his mission was urgent. The British would have captured the patriots' weapons unless he could warn the minutemen.*

REVOLUTION, AMERICAN

The American Revolution, or Revolutionary War (1775–1783), was fought between Great Britain and its 13 American colonies. The American victory resulted in the independence of the United States of America.

The causes of the American Revolution were both political and economic. For the most part the American colonies were self-governing. But after the British defeated the French in the French and Indian War (1754–1763), the British did many things to assert their control. They decided to station large numbers of troops in the colonies—and to make the colonists pay for this. They also tried to prevent the colonists from settling on land west of the Appalachian Mountains. They told the colonists they could trade only with the British. And they passed such acts as the STAMP ACT. It seemed to the Americans that the British were trying to govern the colonies for the benefit of Britain—not the colonies.

American anger deepened when a number of them were killed by British troops in the BOSTON MASSACRE in 1770. When the British placed a tax on tea, the colonists responded with the BOSTON TEA PARTY, in which British tea was destroyed. To punish the Americans, the British passed what the colonies called the "Intolerable Acts" in 1774. One of these acts closed the port of Boston.

▲ The Americans defeated British General John Burgoyne near Saratoga, New York, on October 17, 1777. Burgoyne and his 6,000 Redcoats had been trying to cut off New England from the other colonies. The victory convinced France to support the American cause.

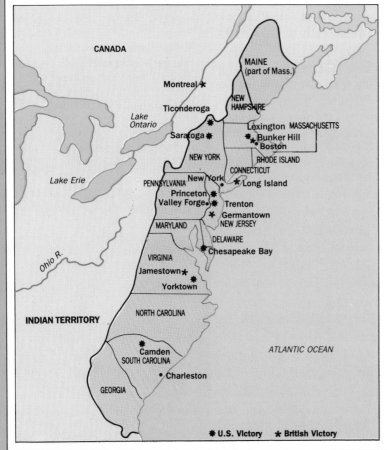

George Washington was an excellent choice for commander of the Continental Army. Until his appointment, most of the fighting had been confined to the state of Massachusetts. With General Washington, a Virginian, in overall command, the Americans could prove that the Revolution had united both northern and southern colonies in their dispute with the British.

The colonists now convened the First CONTINENTAL CONGRESS. They denounced the British laws and said they would not trade with Britain. Most colonists wanted fairness, but not independence. Nevertheless, colonial militias were formed. When the British sent troops to destroy the militias' arms at Concord, Massachusetts, the Americans fought back. The battles of LEXINGTON AND CONCORD marked the beginning of the American Revolution.

In July 1775, the Second Continental Congress named George WASHINGTON commander of the Continental Army. A year later, on July 4, 1776, the DECLARATION OF INDEPENDENCE was adopted.

Many battles were fought, with neither side gaining a definite advantage. The turning point came in 1778, when France signed an alliance with the United States and sent troops and ships to help. The British commander, Lord Charles Cornwallis, was forced to surrender to American forces at Yorktown, Virginia, on October 19, 1781. There was little fighting after this, and on September 3, 1793, under the terms of the Treaty of Paris, Britain recognized the independence of the United States of America.

Major Battles of the American Revolution

1775 The American Revolution starts with the battles of Lexington and Concord (April 19). The British win the Battle of Bunker Hill (June 17).

1776 The colonists are forced to retreat from Long Island (August 27). The patriots win a major victory at Trenton, New Jersey (December 26).

1777 The British suffer heavy losses near Bennington, Vermont (August 16). The British win the Battle of Brandywine and occupy nearby Philadelphia (September 11). The British win the Battle of Germantown, Pennsylvania (October 4).

1779 Victory at Vincennes enables the Americans to gain control of most of the Northwest Territory (February 25).

1780 The British capture Charleston, South Carolina (May 12).

1781 The British suffer a major defeat at Cowpens, South Carolina (January 17). The British surrender at Yorktown, Virginia, virtually ending the American Revolution (October 19).

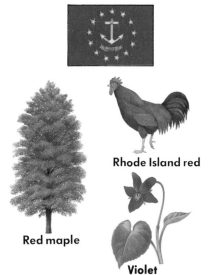

Rhode Island red

Red maple

Violet

Places of Interest

- Newport is a leading resort center. It offers swimming, boating, and fishing. Also in Newport is the beautiful Cliff Walk, a 3-mile (5-km) path that passes by the seaside mansions and along the coast of the Atlantic Ocean.
- Block Island, 10 miles (16 km) off the mainland, is a famous resort area.
- Slater Mill, in Pawtucket, was one of the first textile mills in North America. The mill is now a museum.

Rhode Island is one of the six NEW ENGLAND states. It borders Connecticut on the west, Massachusetts on the north and east, and the Atlantic Ocean on the south. Its nickname is the Ocean State. Rhode Island is the smallest state. And its population density is second highest in the nation. Providence, with a population of 160,000, is the largest city and capital. It is located in the eastern part of the state, at the head of Narragansett Bay.

Rhode Island was founded in 1636 by Roger WILLIAMS. He had been expelled from the colony of Massachusetts for promoting religious and political freedom. In May 1776, Rhode Island became the first colony to formally declare its independence from England. But it was the last of the 13 original colonies to join the Union.

The new state of Rhode Island developed the textile industry that had begun during Colonial times. With the large markets of New York City and Boston nearby, the factory towns of Pawtucket, Woonsocket, Cranston, and Warwick prospered. The manufacture of textiles is still important to Rhode Island. The state's other products include jewelry, silverware, machinery, metal goods, and rubber products.

Tourism is also important to Rhode Island. The islands in Narragansett Bay, and the area around the bay, are known for their beautiful beaches. The city of Newport, with its magnificent seaside mansions, attracts many visitors. There are more than 300 colonial buildings in the city. One of them, Touro Synagogue, is the oldest synagogue in the United States.

◄ Sport fishing is popular in the Ocean State. The waters off Rhode Island provide large fish such as tuna (left), as well as smaller fish such as mackerel, bluefish, and bass.

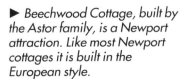

▲ America's richest families built summer homes along the coast in Newport, Rhode Island, at the turn of the century. These houses are called "cottages" but are really huge mansions.

Woonsocket •
295
Pawtucket
Providence •
△
Jerimoth Hill
812 ft (247 m)
Scituate Res.
Cranston •
Flat River Res.
95
Warwick
Narragansett Bay
Rhode Island
Rhode Island Sound
Middletown
Newport

0   10 miles
0   10 kilometers

ATLANTIC OCEAN

Block Island

Rhode Island
Capital: Providence
Area: 1,055 sq mi (2,732 km²). Rank: 50th
Population: 1,005,984 (1990). Rank: 43rd
Statehood: May 29, 1790
Principal rivers: Blackstone, Providence
Highest point: Jerimoth Hill, 812 ft (247 m)
Motto: Hope
Song: "Rhode Island"

▶ Beechwood Cottage, built by the Astor family, is a Newport attraction. Like most Newport cottages it is built in the European style.

RICKENBACKER, Eddie

Edward ("Eddie") Rickenbacker (1890–1978) was a World War I fighter pilot and later an airline executive. He was born in Columbus, Ohio. His first interest was in automobiles and car racing. He joined the U.S. Army during World War I and became the country's leading ace pilot, shooting down 22 enemy planes. After leaving the Army, he went back to working with racing cars—he owned the famous Indianapolis Speedway. From 1938 to 1963 he was president and then chairman of the board of Eastern Airlines. During World War II, Rickenbacker was an adviser to the government.

RIDE, Sally

Sally Ride (1951–) was the first American woman to travel in space. Born in Los Angeles, she received a Ph.D. in physics from Stanford University in 1977 and soon became an astronaut. In 1983 she rocketed into space aboard the space shuttle *Challenger*. A year later she made another flight on the shuttle. In both flights important experiments were carried out by the crew. In 1987, Ride left the space program to accept a position with Stanford.

▲ *Eddie Rickenbacker was the leading American combat pilot in World War I. He shot down 22 enemy airplanes and 4 observation balloons.*

▼ *Louis Riel's two uprisings led to his execution for treason in 1884. Many Canadians now view him as a hero who fought for the rights of native-born Canadians.*

RIEL, Louis

Louis Riel (1844–1885) led two rebellions against the Canadian government. Born in St. Boniface, Manitoba, he was a méti, a person of mixed white and Indian ancestry. He and his followers fought to prevent their land from being taken over by new settlers. In 1869 he led the First Riel Rebellion, also known as the Red River Rebellion. Canadian soldiers forced Riel to flee. In 1885 the métis turned to Riel for help again, after they had moved to what is now Saskatchewan. Once again Canadian soldiers defeated Riel. He was captured and hanged.

RIO GRANDE

The Rio Grande is the fifth longest RIVER in North America. It flows for 1,760 miles (2,832 km), forming the entire boundary between Texas and Mexico. The river begins on the CONTINENTAL DIVIDE in the

ROCKY MOUNTAINS of Colorado. It flows through the spectacular Rio Grande Gorge, then through New Mexico and along the Texas border to the GULF OF MEXICO. One of the wildest areas of the United States is found along the Big Bend of the river in Big Bend National Park.

▲ The Rio Grande forms the boundary between Texas and Mexico.

◄ The Rio Grande is one of the longest rivers in North America, but it is too shallow to navigate. It has cut deep canyons into the surrounding cliffs over hundreds of thousands of years.

RIVERS

From Colonial times until the present, rivers in the United States have served as avenues of transportation. Rivers also provide water for farmland, for industry, and for drinking. Waterfalls and dams along rivers provide the power for hydroelectricity.

The longest river system in the United States is the MISSISSIPPI-MISSOURI RIVER SYSTEM. It drains the vast interior of the country and empties into the GULF OF MEXICO. Another major river, the RIO GRANDE, also flows into the Gulf of Mexico. The rivers of the West, such as the COLORADO RIVER and COLUMBIA RIVER, flow into the Pacific Ocean or one of its arms. In the East, such rivers as the HUDSON RIVER and the Potomac River empty into the Atlantic Ocean. One of the most important rivers in the East is the St. Lawrence. The river makes up part of the ST. LAWRENCE SEAWAY, which connects the GREAT LAKES with the Atlantic Ocean.

Longest U.S. Rivers (miles/km)	
1.	Mississippi (2,340/3,766)
2.	Missouri (2,315/3,725)
3.	Rio Grande (1,760/2,832)
4.	Arkansas (1,459/2,348)
5	Colorado (1,450/2,333)
6.	Ohio (1,310/2,108)
7.	Red (1,290/2,076)
8.	Columbia (1,243/2,000)
9.	Snake (1,038/1,670)
10.	Pecos (926/1,490)

The first automobile trip across the United States took more than two months in 1903. Nowadays, using interstate highways, the same 2,934-mile (4,722-km) ride from San Francisco to New York City would take less than a week.

ROADS AND HIGHWAYS

There are almost 3.9 million miles (6.3 million km) of roads and highways in the United States. Most of these roads are under state or local control. The federal government pays some or all of the funds for those highways called Federally Aided Highways. Among them are interstate highways. There are 44,000 miles (71,000 km) of interstate highways in the United States. About 90 percent of all U.S. roads are surfaced. Texas has more roads (286,000 miles, or 460,000 km) than any other state in the nation. Hawaii, with 4,100 miles (6,600 km), has the least.

▶ A freeway junction at San Jose, California, appears as a geometric design when seen from the air.

ROBESON, Paul

Paul Robeson (1898–1976) was a singer, actor, and civil rights advocate. Born in Princeton, New Jersey, he graduated from Rutgers University. He also earned a law degree from Columbia University but soon turned to acting. Robeson became famous for his performance in the title role of Eugene O'Neill's play *The Emperor Jones*. His beautiful bass-baritone voice created a memorable interpretation of the song "Ol' Man River" in Jerome Kern's *Showboat*. He also appeared on radio and made records and movies.

After World War II, Robeson fought for civil rights for blacks. But his friendship with the Soviet Union resulted in a campaign against him. For many years he lived and worked in Europe.

▼ Paul Robeson played the title role in the 1943 production of Othello, which ran for a record 196 performances. His acting in this play earned him several awards.

 The robin is one of North America's hardiest birds. Crocus blossoms of early spring welcome this robin after a winter searching for food.

ROBIN

One of the best-known North American birds, the American robin is a type of thrush. It is about 10 inches (25 cm) long and has a beautiful song. The male has a rust-colored breast; the female's coloring is less bright. It breeds all over North America. Robins from northern regions usually fly south in winter. The robin builds its nest in a tree or sometimes a barn or other building. A pair will rear two or even three broods in the spring and summer. The robin eats berries, insects, and worms.

The first English settlers in Colonial America gave the robin its name. Seeing a local bird with red markings on its chest, they were reminded of the English robin, or robin redbreast. However, the two birds are unrelated; the English robin is only about half the size of the American robin.

ROBINSON, Edwin Arlington

Edwin Arlington Robinson (1869–1935) was an important poet of the early 20th century. He won three Pulitzer Prizes. Many of his early works were about unhappy people, such as "Luke Havergal," "Richard Cory," and "Miniver Cheevy." In 1921 his *Collected Poems* won the first Pulitzer Prize for poetry. Among his works from these later years are several long narrative poems based on the King Arthur legends: *Merlin*, *Lancelot*, and *Tristram*.

▼ Edwin Arlington Robinson's first volumes of poetry contain character sketches of townspeople from an imaginary place called Tilbury Town. The community is based on the town of Gardiner, Maine, where Robinson had lived as a child.

ROBINSON, Jackie

Jack Roosevelt (Jackie) Robinson (1919–1972) was the first black to play baseball in the major leagues. Born in Cairo, Georgia, he attended the University of California. There he starred in baseball, football, basketball, and track. After college, Robinson played in baseball's minor leagues. In 1947, Robinson joined the Brooklyn

▲ *The father-and-son team of John D. Rockefeller, Sr. and Jr., represented a large proportion of America's wealth.*

John D. Rockefeller, Sr., was the son of a peddler. At the age of 16 he started work in a small produce firm. He entered the oil business at 23 and became the world's richest man before he was 40. He gave away $550 million during his lifetime.

▶ *Rockefeller Center, in New York City, comes ablaze each year with its Christmas decorations.*

Dodgers as a second baseman and was named the National League's rookie of the year. During his ten years with the Dodgers, they won six pennants and one World Series. He was elected to the National Baseball Hall of Fame in 1962.

ROCKEFELLER FAMILY

The Rockefeller family is noted for its activities in business, politics, and philanthropy. John D. Rockefeller, Sr. (1839–1937), founded the Standard Oil Company in 1870. By 1882 his company controlled most of the oil business in the United States, and he became a multimillionaire. He and his descendants contributed much of their fortune to good causes. For example, a gift from John D. Rockefeller, Sr., made possible the founding of the University of Chicago. His son, John D. Rockefeller, Jr. (1874–1960), funded the restoration of Colonial Williamsburg, Virginia.

John D. Rockefeller, Jr., had five sons. John D. Rockefeller III (1906–1978) helped create Lincoln Center in New York City. Nelson Rockefeller (1908–1979) was a governor of New York and vice

president under Gerald Ford. Lawrence Rockefeller (1910–) is an active conservationist. Winthrop Rockefeller (1912–1973) was a governor of Arkansas. David Rockefeller (1915–) was the head of Chase Manhattan Bank. Among the other noted Rockefellers is John D. Rockefeller IV (1937–), who has served as West Virginia governor and U.S. senator.

ROCKETS AND MISSILES

A rocket is a kind of engine. Rockets burn fuel that turns into hot gases. As the gases expand, they shoot out of the open end of the rocket, and the rocket is pushed forward. Rockets are used to launch artificial satellites, manned spacecraft, space probes, and military missiles.

The Chinese invented rockets in the 1200s. During World War II, the Germans built rockets to bombard London. After the war, the German rocket scientist Wernher VON BRAUN led a team that helped the United States to build the first Saturn rocket. A Saturn V rocket was used to send the first man to the moon. The space shuttle uses rockets to achieve space orbit.

Rockets are used to launch military missiles. Some missiles can travel up to 5,000 miles (8,000 km).

▲ A U.S. Navy Harpoon missile is launched from the U.S.S. New Jersey. Missile boats can carry up to eight guided missiles that can be fired accurately at distant targets.

▶ More than nine tenths of a rocket is discarded after it projects its capsule into orbit. Huge amounts of thrust are needed to achieve the speed necessary to gain earth orbit.

▶ *Chuck Berry became one of the first rock music stars. His energetic singing and guitar playing has influenced many other performers.*

▼ *Elvis Presley rose from his poor Mississippi childhood to become the world's best-known singer.*

▼ *Madonna has entered the 1990s as one of the rock world's most popular performers. Her records and movie appearances have made her a star around the world.*

ROCK MUSIC

Rock music is the most popular type of music in the United States and in many other countries. The term "rock" is short for "rock and roll." The music's fast, strong beat has a strong appeal for young people.

Rock and roll developed in the mid-1950s. It was a mixture of black rhythm and blues music and country and western music. The first rock stars, such as Little Richard and Chuck Berry, had already been playing their music in black nightclubs. They were joined by white singers such as Bill Haley, Elvis Presley, and Buddy Holly in the late 1950s. The Beatles, an English group, widened the appeal of rock when they first visited the United States in 1964.

During the 1960s, rock music was the music of protest. It was taken up by people in the civil rights movement and by anti–Vietnam War protesters. Its popularity was evident when 500,000 people attended a three-day rock festival at Woodstock, New York, in 1969.

In recent years, rock has gone through many changes. It no longer has one sound. Folk rock, country rock, soul rock, punk rock, and other forms attract different audiences. And rock stars, such as Michael Jackson, Madonna, Bon Jovi, Prince, and New Kids on the Block, continue to sell millions of records.

ROCKNE, Knute

Knute Rockne (1888–1931) was one of the greatest college football coaches in the United States. Born in Norway, he came to the United States with his parents when he was five years old. He studied chemistry at the University of Notre Dame and played on the school's football team. In 1918, Rockne became the coach of the Notre Dame football team. Between then and 1931 his team won 105 games, lost 12, and tied 5. The team went five seasons without a single defeat. Rockne's *Autobiography* was published in 1931, soon after he died in a plane crash.

▲ *Knute Rockne's football teams at Notre Dame University built their fearsome reputations on tough practice and loyalty. Rockne introduced many modern coaching techniques to the sport.*

ROCKWELL, Norman

Norman Rockwell (1894–1978) was a famous illustrator. He is best known for the covers he painted for the *Saturday Evening Post*. Over a period of half a century he produced 317 *Post* covers, depicting scenes of small town and family life with sympathetic humor and a wealth of realistic detail. Rockwell's first illustrations were done for children's magazines such as *Boy's Life* and *St. Nicholas*.

During World War II, Rockwell's paintings representing the Four Freedoms (freedom of speech and religion and freedom from want and fear) were reproduced and distributed throughout the United States.

▼ *Norman Rockwell's* The County Agricultural Agent *shows the artist's ability to capture everyday life in a realistic and understanding way.*

ROCKY MOUNTAINS

The Rocky Mountains form the largest mountain system in North America. They stretch for 3,000 miles (4,800 km), from New Mexico in the south to Alaska in the north. There are five major sections of the Rockies. The Southern, Central, and Northern Rockies are in the United States. The Canadian Rockies are in Canada. The Brooks Range is in Alaska. The crest of the Rockies forms the CONTINENTAL DIVIDE.

There are more than 50 Rocky Mountain peaks that are more than 14,000 feet (4,300 m) above sea level. The highest, Mount Elbert (14,431 feet, or 4,399 m), is in Colorado. Many rivers rise in the Rockies, including the COLORADO, COLUMBIA, Missouri, and RIO GRANDE.

During the early 1800s, the LEWIS AND CLARK expedition and Zebulon PIKE and other explorers crossed the Rockies. But the mountains were a barrier to American westward expansion. Among the first people to live there were fur traders. In the mid-1800s, prospectors flocked to the Rockies to search for gold.

Today gold, silver, lead, coal, copper, and other minerals are mined in the Rockies. Lumbering is another important industry, as is tourism. Each year, hundreds of thousands of people visit the Rockies to fish, hunt, hike, and ski and to explore the beauty of the many national parks in the mountains. United States parks include YELLOWSTONE, Mesa Verde, GRAND CANYON, Grand Teton, Rocky Mountain, and Bryce Canyon. Canada's Rocky Mountain national parks include Banff, Jasper, and Kootenay.

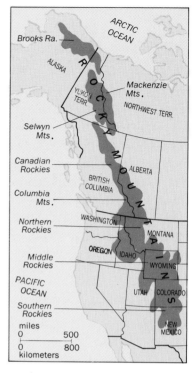

▲ The Rocky Mountains are made up of several ranges, from the Southern Rockies to the Brooks Range, which extends north of the Arctic Circle.

◀ Ear Mountain is typical of the Rocky Mountains of Montana. The terrain is well above the tree line, and only hardy grasses grow by the cold lakes.

The Rocky Mountains were the most daunting obstacle facing the pioneers on their way west. Settlements had been established in the Great Plains as early as 1810, but it took more than 50 years for the Oregon Trail to open a route through the Rocky Mountains.

▼ The Teton Range in Wyoming is one of the most spectacular sections of the Rockies. Grand Teton National Park features dramatic mountain scenery and giant glaciers.

▲ Rodents use their long front teeth to gnaw through nuts and wood for food and shelter.

RODENTS

Rodents are mammals that have front teeth that are ideal for gnawing. There are more rodents than any other kind of mammal in the world. In North America, rodents include the BEAVER, CHIPMUNK, gerbil, GOPHER, GROUNDHOG, GROUND SQUIRREL, guinea pig, hamster, MOUSE, MUSKRAT, PACK RAT, PORCUPINE, PRAIRIE DOG, RAT, and SQUIRREL.

Many rodents, such as the gopher, groundhog, and prairie dog, live in burrows in the ground. A few, such as the beaver and muskrat, live in fresh water.

RODEO

A rodeo is a form of entertainment and a sporting event for cowboys and cowgirls, who demonstrate their riding and roping skills. There are five main events in rodeos: bareback bronc riding, saddle bronc riding, bull riding, calf roping, and steer wrestling, or bulldogging. Another event, a horse race known as barrel racing, is primarily for cowgirls. In all-girl rodeos, however, the cowgirls compete in bareback bronc riding, bull riding, calf roping, and other events.

A major U.S. rodeo is the National Finals Rodeo in Oklahoma City, Oklahoma. The Stampede in Calgary, Alberta, is Canada's most important rodeo.

▼ The All Indian Rodeo in Tygh Valley, Oregon. Team roping is one of the main events of the rodeo.